the PUNT & DENNIS INSTANT LIBRARY

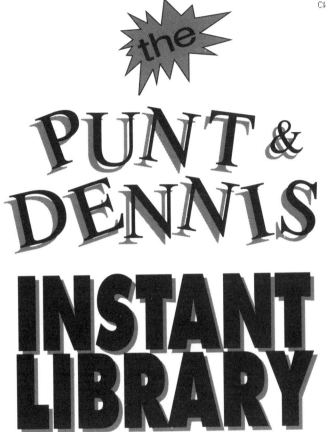

First published in Great Britain in 1993 by
Fourth Estate Limited
289 Westbourne Grove
London W11 2QA

A catalogue record for this book is available from the British Library.

ISBN 1–85702–163–0

Designed and Typeset by Button Design Company.
Printed in Great Britain by Clays Ltd, St Ives plc

All characters referred to in the text and in photographs are entirely fictitious.

CONTENTS

"The best-selling guide to *real* gardening."

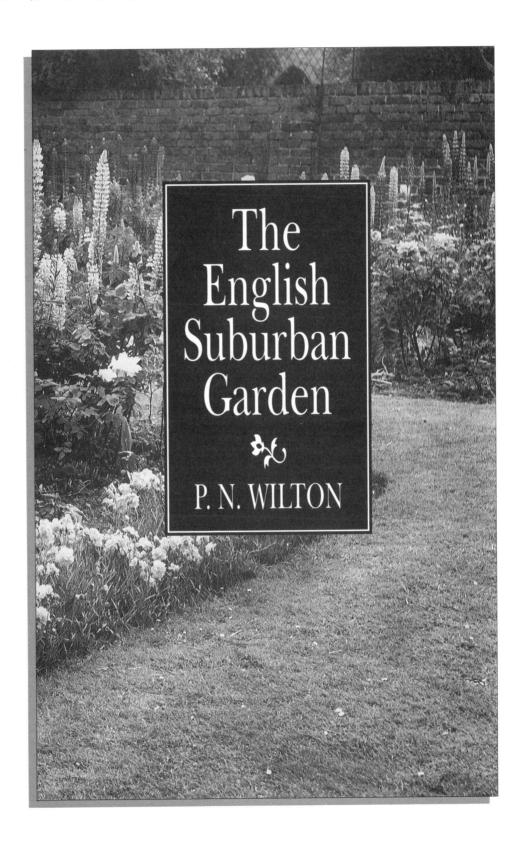

The
English
Suburban
Garden

P. N. WILTON

The English
Suburban Garden

INTRODUCTION
by Lady Lavinia Broxbourne-Thackett

"A garden is a lovesome thing, God wot." God wot? Actually, in the 17th century, "wot" meant "to know", so the phrase means "Lord knows how thoroughly jolly a nice garden is." But I wouldn't expect any of you ghastly plebs to know that. And that's the whole purpose of this little book. Because, goodness me, don't you get tired of all those gardening books which feature enormous country gardens? Well, I don't, obviously – I've got an enormous country garden myself, 48 acres of Hampshire actually. But most of you oiks out there have probably got a pathetic little strip of lawn out the back of your boxy little residence in some hideous sprawling suburban town, and there are no gardening books for you.

There's no point telling you how to lay out a rhododendron grove to draw the eye to a formal water-feature, or how to construct a pergola, or how to plant a shrubbery, because you simply haven't the room, my dears. So that is why I said I would write the introduction to *The English Suburban Garden* (well, that plus the large cheque I was offered) because this is the first book which is actually aimed at *real, ordinary gardens*. There is no reason whatsoever why the lack of a tennis court, or croquet lawn, or woodland, should impede you from enjoying your garden. So read on, and enjoy!

CHAPTER ONE

Basic Layout

When Capability Brown laid out the grounds of Blenheim Palace in the mid-18th century, he designed the sweeping vista down to the lake, the elegant positioning of the trees, the dramatic contrasts of foliage and flower, but he never put in anywhere for the Duke's children to play football.

It is essential, in the first stages of designing your garden, to remember that *whatever you do, your kids will ruin it anyway*. It is therefore best, if you have children, to abandon any thoughts of formal planting and concentrate instead on re-inforcing your fencing and giving all possible protection to windows.

There are certain varieties of hardy plant which will stand up to suburban children, principally BUSH ROSES. These are very spiky and children will swiftly learn, after sufficient lacerations, blood loss and tetanus jabs, to avoid going near them. Certain strains of rose bushes (such as the *Lady Hamilton*, the *MacMillan's Delight* and the *Schwarzenegger*) will also develop spines strong enough to puncture a stray football. This can prove very useful against predators, not to mention friends of your kids who you don't like.

It is therefore best, if you really must sprog, to abandon any thoughts of plants and stick instead to Garden Features. Many a garden, for example, will benefit from the addition of a SAND PIT, while the eye cannot fail to be drawn by a focal item such as a RUSTY SWING, or *Deathtrappus lethallus*. This type of garden is really seen at its best in high summer, which brings the cheerful blue colouring of the CRAPPY PADDLING POOL (*Inflatus argoscatalogue*). This can spread up to six feet across and, left in place long enough during a hot spell, will irrevocably kill all the grass underneath it (if any).

Variety, careful design and adventurous planting help make full use of space

CHAPTER TWO

Social Climbers

In addition to ground-cover, annuals, perennials and shrubs, no garden is really complete without some of the more common social climbers. These simple additions can make even the most mediocre strip of heavily shaded, fenced-in suburban ground look like a mediocre, fenced-in strip of suburban ground with some pretentious accessories in it.

1. GNOMES

Much has been written about garden gnomes. Those with no sense of irony regard them as the *sine qua non* of suburban tastelessness: tacky, hideous and irredeemably naff in absolutely every way. There is another school of thought, that of post-modernist semiotics, which regards them as iconographic objects of ultimate kitsch – in other words: tacky, hideous and irretrievably naff in absolutely every way. There is a third school of thought which simply says that if you can look at a garden gnome without puking up, you are a hopeless case.

However, one may take the fashionable view that their very reputation makes gnomes a very trendy accessory; that young couples, showing their superior sense of bourgeois irony, buy gnomes with a knowing nod to the tackiness they embody. The technical term for such people is *crap people*. You know the sort – they put up with some rubbishy old radio just because its "so Fifties" and make their tea with some ancient old kettle that doesn't switch itself off, because *The Face* once had a picture of it labelled "Post-War Lifestyle Icon". Do not, repeat DO NOT, be intimidated by these people. If they ever say to you "of course, the garden gnome is a whimsical joke on our part," just reply, "you are crap people". That'll sort 'em out.

Look at these cheerful little fellows

2. BARBECUES

Summer invariably brings the flowering of the Common Home Barbecue, or *Listeria maximus*. These provide a fine visual focus and will serve to attract such useful little garden creatures as moths, mice, rats and stray dogs. They should be put in a shady position, giving ample space for the smoke to fill the garden and to allow the wind to blow it out. They are easily maintained, requiring only a bag of charcoal briquettes (available on any garage forecourt) and four gallons of lighting fluid.

The principal drawback of a barbecue is that it will not cook food, except in geological time. A rough guide to cooking times is given below:

FOOD TYPE	COOKING TIME
Small sausage	4 - 6 hours
Large sausage	12 hours
Chicken leg	1.5 days
Steak (rare)	2 weeks
Steak (medium)	1 calendar month
Steak (well-done)	6 months

3. WATER FEATURES

The grounds of a country estate would often contain rivers or streams whose course could be diverted by a skilful landscape gardener to create waterfalls, ponds and ornamental lakes. These water features can easily be duplicated in the suburban garden by means of a fibreglass kidney-bowl-shaped thingy in bright blue, or, easier still, digging a hole and lining it with polythene. You then pour in some water, add some weed and a frog or two, and hey presto! You have a stagnant pool of foul water.

More ambitious designers can opt for a fountain, perhaps pouring through the mouth of a griffin or flying out of the outstretched arm of the Venus de Milo, tastefully modelled in Roc-U-Like, the moulded high-density-plastic stone-substitute that really looks like the real thing, only isn't. Such fountains are driven by a small electric pump, and on a hot summer day what could be more pleasant than to be lulled by the musical sound of falling water and the faint background hum of an electric pump-mechanism? Many people like to add goldfish, perhaps to see how long it takes them to die (usually, about a week).

The important thing, when designing a water-feature, is that it should ideally look *utterly wrong* when set in the context of the overall garden.

4. ROCKERY

A rockery is what it says it is: a self-contained eco-system, a small corner of your garden where, suddenly, climatic and soil conditions are different, enabling different species of plants – shallow-rooting Alpines and scree-growing rarities – to flower in a habitat close to their own. No? Oh, all right then – it's a load of rocks chucked in a corner.

CHAPTER THREE

Planting

Sometimes, people who grow tired of swings, paddling pools, bicycles, spacehoppers, sun-loungers, barbecues, patios, parasol-tables and so on will opt for a radical and highly unusual design-scheme for their garden: they will fill it with green, oddly shaped objects which "grow" through the course of the year.

These objects are known as "plants", and come in various different types. The two principal varieties are known as "live" plants and "dead" plants. For most people, the bulk of their experience will be with the latter, so let's look at these first.

A beautiful mixed border. Yours will look nothing like this

Dead Plants

Any typical suburban garden will probably contain a variety of dead plants, each with their own unique character and smell. It is important to distinguish between *Dead Annuals* and *Dead Perennials*. A dead annual is just something that was supposed to grow this year but hasn't. A dead perennial will last for much longer, standing brown and shrivelled for years to come.

In planning your dead plants, try to achieve a nice balance between types. Some plants will struggle for weeks, while others simply die overnight, apparently for no reason. The careful suburban gardener can achieve a nice brown-and-green effect by planting the two types together.

The keys to a good display of dead plants are:

1. PLANTING IN THE WRONG PLACE

Some plants won't grow in the shade, and others don't like the sun. A sun-loving plant, planted in the shade, will be stunted and discoloured, while a shade-loving plant placed in direct sunlight will go brown and die. For the best results, make sure you ignore the instructions on the label, and plant things wherever you feel like it at the time. This will ensure a vigorous, healthy plant for at least 48 hours or so.

2. ATTACK BY PESTS

There is a more detailed section on pests below but, for now, it is enough to remember that aphids, flies, slugs and snails will, given the opportunity, eat everything you plant. If your plants look vigorous and healthy, then you don't have enough pests.

3. FAILING TO WATER

This is a simple but very effective way to make your garden look truly suburban. The true suburban gardener sticks a plant in the flower bed and then leaves it alone. He doesn't pander to the bloody thing by giving it water. I mean, it's a plant, isn't it? Let it wait for the rain like it's supposed to. If you mollycoddle it, it'll become weak and prone to disease. If you really must water your plants, thus showing what an anal-retentive neurotic you are, then make sure you just sprinkle them enough to wet the topsoil. A plant that dies just because it hasn't rained for a few days is a plant that doesn't deserve to live anyway, I say.

4. PLANTING AT WRONG TIME OF YEAR, IN WRONG SOIL

A lot of plants are completely namby-pamby and can't cope with anything. They have to have special soil, exactly the right temperature, and generally are right little primadonna-ish little bastards. Lots of plants – fuchsias, for example – must not be planted too early, or they can become frost-damaged and die. The thing to do here is *talk* to your plants. Say to them, "get out there and grow, you big girl's blouse." Furthermore, camellias, rhododendrons, and various other common plants require ericaceous soil. The true suburban gardener plants them anyway, and watches them shrivel.

5. NO-APPARENT-REASON SYNDROME

Known as NARS, this is usually the reason for a dead plant. You can follow all the instructions, you can do it all right, and the plant, ungrateful little bastard that it is, just shrivels up and dies. There's nothing you can do about it.

7

Live Plants

Sometimes, despite the best efforts of the suburban gardener, a plant will remain alive, and may, in extreme cases, even grow and flower. If a plant shows signs of developing such "flowers" then the most important thing to remember is: DO NOT PANIC. This is not a sign of failure. It is merely nature taking its course. All you can do is allow it to happen, and learn your lessons for another year.

Tell-tale signs that a plant may be healthy are that it will increase in size as the summer goes on. You will notice rounded ends, or "buds", developing, and after a while these will open into brightly coloured arrangments of petals. These are the "flowers". If any of your plants do this, there are steps you can take to minimize the problem.

Firstly, do not cut any of the flowers. Leave them *in situ* to go brown and fall off. This encourages the plant to stop flowering. Secondly, if the plant is in good light, consider moving it to under a tree. Another course of action is to accidentally chop it down with the lawn-mower, or to light a bonfire near it and scorch it. Thirdly, do not, on any account, do any weeding. Weeds are the suburban gardener's friend and ally, and a good display of really fine weeds will choke any flowers which try and grow through them.

I have visited some of the finest weed-gardens in England, and a glorious sight they make. The grounds of 34 Tarbie Avenue, Cheam, for example (open 10am–5pm, May–September) contain some of the biggest weeds grown in temperate climates. The owners, Alan and May Brownlow, have painstakingly neglected their collection of weeds since they bought the house over 12 years ago, and the resulting luxuriant foliage of knotted, tangled greenery is a joy to the eye. Derek Kettley's garden at 46 Johnson Crescent, Reading, has been listed by Friends of the Earth as an Area of Special Scientific Interest. Apart from the many tons of carbon dioxide which Derek's garden absorbs, it is also believed to contain over half the world's species of weed, including many unknown to science. These rich, lush environments provide a home for many hundreds of animals, including the rat, vole, fox, stray cat, louse and tramp. It will be a tragedy for the human race if, in our rush to clear these weeds in order to grow sterile rows of marigolds and geraniums, we lose an irreplaceable natural resource before we have had time to fully exploit its riches. Last year in Hemel Hempstead, for example, biologists found a species of weed which contains a chemical believed to help relieve the symptoms of rheumatism, and are excited that another recently discovered weed, found at the back of a garden of a student house in Greater Manchester, will yield a cure for cancer, provide a new protein source that can relieve world starvation, and also be trained to change channels on the TV for you.

Pests

Of the many problems that render gardening such a depressing and frustrating pastime, the worst of all is PESTS. These consist of every other living thing in the world apart from you, none of whom want your plants to grow. This includes birds, which will peck up freshly sown seeds; snails and slugs, which will eat leaves and stems; foxes, dogs and cats, which will dig up young plants; and the grumpy pensioners next door, who feel, like all old people, that they're the only ones who have any right to a nice garden.

Let's take some of these pests in turn:

1. CATS

Cats are a pest for one reason – they dig up your flowerbeds and shit in them. It's only one reason, but it's a pretty good one. The first option is to try REPELLENTS such as "Pepper Dust", which cats do not like. These are available from any garden centre. They are cheap, easy to use, and not harmful to children. Their only drawback is that they do not work. Ever. There is an old gardener's expression: "Put down dust beside your wall/ It will do precisely bugger all."

The household on the left are true Suburban Gardeners

The second option is to use NETTING attached to canes driven firmly into the ground. Be sure to attach the bottom of the netting securely with tent-pegs. What will then happen is that the cat will either go round the side or wriggle underneath, and then shit in your flowerbed.

A third solution, which many people opt for, is to purchase a ferocious DOG, perhaps a Rottweiler or Alsatian, then chain it up and starve it for several weeks, and finally dangle raw meat under its nose to give it a taste for blood. After a few months of this, when the dog has begun to slaver and its eyes are glazed with psychotic hatred of any living thing, unchain it and watch it ignore the cat and savage next-door's toddler instead. This may not matter, since next-door's toddler may well have shat in your flowerbed as well.

Some gardeners find that that the only really foolproof solution to the problem of cats is LAND-MINES, sited at intervals along the edge of flower-borders. These can be hard to find at Sainsbury's Homebase or your local garden centre, but can be obtained through Ahmed El-Ferraz International Import-Export Ltd, 43A Dubious Crescent, London W2. They cost approximately £1500 each (conventional) or £2,400 (nuclear) but you'll get a discount for bulk-buying, and it's well worth it to see those pesky moggies splatter all over the fence! Ensure that you place a large warning notice in the vicinity, and you will sleep better at night knowing your plants are safe. Occasionally, you may be woken up by a huge explosion, but generally, you will sleep better.

2. SNAILS AND SLUGS

These creatures - gastropods - really are the bane of any gardener's life, and have been for centuries. The Earl of Huntingdon wrote in 1628 that "the beautye of the Garden is Spoyled by the Intrusion of the Ravening Snayle and Slugge, which, by their Appetites do Render the Leaves full of Holes, and which Truly are to be Trodd'n on." The Earl's forthright views were echoed a century later by the early Georgian poet and gardener, Alexander Barret, who wrote in his *Elegy Upon The Flowers* that:

> *Now, as Spring doth cast her robes aside,*
> *The joys of Summer coyly to reveal,*
> *What slimy canker crawls upon the earth,*
> *Why, 'tis the glistening wake of Mr Snayle!*
> *That Vile Slime, by which, if we should follow,*
> *Will lead us to this Villain in his Shell*
> *Upon a Hosta sits this Hungry Horror,*
> *And all his fellow-Parasites as Well.*
> *The Leaves they lie in tatters, all are Shredded*
> *The flower-bud is eaten 'ere tis Pluck'd.*
> *Ah, lament, lament, the coming of the Snayle!*
> *For if he Comes, your garden's Truly fuck'd.*

There is really only one surefire solution to get rid of a snail: pick it up, put it down on a hard surface, and stamp on it very hard until the whole shell is crushed and the slimy slug-bit in the middle is nothing more than a flattened puddle of rubbery mess. Alternatively, you can adopt the French solution and eat it.

3. BIRDS

The best way to deter birds used to be to make a scarecrow, but frankly, modern-day birds are wise to this one. An old overcoat stuck on a pole with a hat on top is not going to frighten your average streetwise urban sparrow. A far better solution is to contact Ahmed El-Ferraz International Import-Export, 43A Dubious Crescent, London W2, who for a modest price will sell you a dozen ground-to-air missiles (or, if you live in a flat, air-to-air missiles) and a shoulder-held launcher. (The DTI know all about these weapons, which were licensed for import as "toilet-roll holder components", although no Government ministers were ever told, and even if they had been, the memo would certainly not have been shredded by MI5. Never.)

4. OLD PEOPLE

Old people are a perennial pest. They always think they know about gardening, and because they've got nothing to do all day, they spend lots of their time peering through their net curtains at *your* garden and moaning that you don't keep it tidy, and you're letting the tone of the neighbourhood down. The only solution is to go round to their house and inform them that the tone of the neighbourhood really shouldn't matter to them since they're going to be dead soon. Furthermore, if they make one more comment about how you don't keep your front garden neat enough, you'll ensure that it's sooner still.

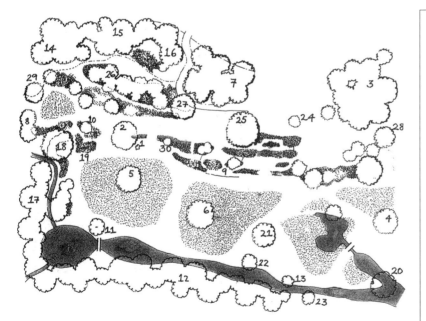

Suggested Planting Plan

1 One Surviving Sweetpea
2 Large Thistle (*Weedus bigbastardus*)
3 Weeds
4 Bushy Thing left by Previous Resident
5 Rosebush (£3.99 special offer at Sainsbury's)
6 Purple Thing
7 Bigger Weeds
8 Struggling Marigolds
9 Slugs
10 Cat-shit
11 Stump of Hosta (eaten by slugs)
12 Orangey Things (*Cheapus gardencentrus*)
13 White Alyssum (*Pieceofpissius evenicangrowius*)
14 Old Man's Beard
15 Old Man's Nasalhair
16 Old Man's Pubes
17 Common Ivy (*Hedera easygrowia*)
18 Love-in-a-mist
19 Dead-in-a-week
20 Gladioli that never came up (*Bulbus deadus*)
21 Hybrid Tea Rose
22 Dog Rose
23 Axl Rose
24 Wild Pansies
25 Huge Weed (*Thingus enormus*)
26 Hydrangea
27 Lonerangea
28 Howdystrangea
29 Floribunda Candulumnum (*Sawiton gardenersworldus*)
30 Next-Door's Football

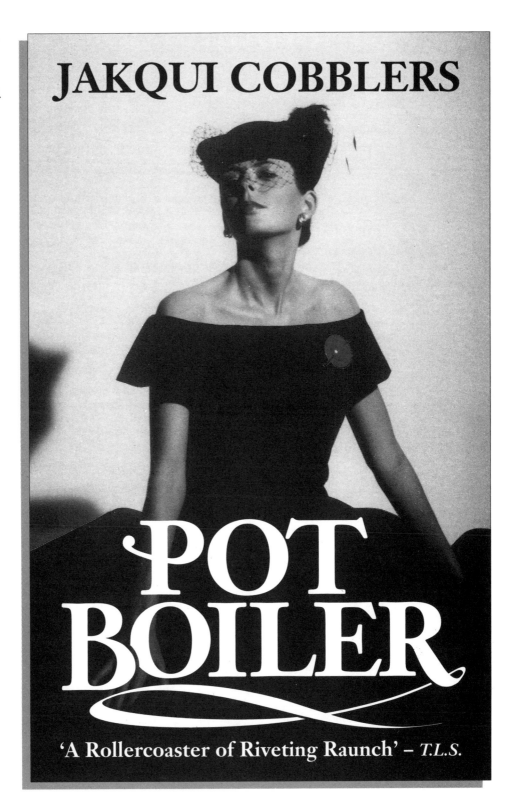

BESTSELLING FICTION

"The sizzling raunch-fest superseller from one of the world's 'biggest unit-shifters'. Soon to be a TV mini-series, almost certainly."

JAKQUI COBBLERS

POT BOILER

'A Rollercoaster of Riveting Raunch' – *T.L.S.*

Zack Mariano, hot property. Hottest young fashion-photographer in the States, Zack lived for kicks and got them. Life in the fast lane. Live fast, die young, that was Zack's motto, and he lived by it. He lived fast, and if he hadn't died young, he was working on it.

"Ok, baby! Yeh! Oh yeh!"

Photo-shoot. Zack's loft-studio in New York. Standing in front of the lights, Josette Carrera, hottest fashion model in the States, fresh from Paris. Mother French, father half-Puerto-Rican, half-Scottish, but all man, and all billionaire. Josette lived for kicks and got them. Live fast, die young, that was her motto, and she lived by it. She lived fast, and if she hadn't died young yet, she was working on it.

"That's right, baby! Lean towards me!"

Josette leans. As she leans her large, firm breasts lean too. Zack thinks "Mmmm!" His 501s tighten. This girl is hot.

Later. Josette's room, the Waldorf Hotel. Silken sheets, champagne in the bucket and clothes on the carpet. Zack's thrusting manhood sending Josette into a nirvana of ecstasy.

"Oh, yes, baby, yes, oh, hot pussy, baby."

"More! More!" she cries.

Later, when the Gods of Love are at last satisfied and Zack sinks exhausted back into the silken sheets, Josette is awake. Goes to the shower. Showers. Water cascades over her firm young body, over her firm young breasts, trickles down her flat firm stomach. As she showers, she thinks. Josette wants more. Modelling is not enough. First-class Concorde from New York to Paris to Milan is not enough. The hundreds of thousands of dollars from her cosmetic endorsements are not enough. Josette wants more. Much more.

She'll do anything to get it. Anything at all.

"Tell him twenty million or it's no deal!"

Loretta Platinum, Head of Programming at ATC, the hottest primetime TV network in the States. Hottest young Head of Network Programming in the States, Loretta lived for kicks and got them. Just 22 years old, gorgeous, blonde, long-legged, Gucci'd – power and sex, a mixture that had every man she met foaming with desire. Loretta had any man she wanted and if they couldn't satisfy her, they were off the network. Last night, one of her top newscasters, Bob Griffin, had collapsed with exhaustion after only her 32nd orgasm. Bob was already fired. Loretta took no shit. Money and sex. That's all there was.

"John?"

Loretta buzzes her PA, John Stallion. Tall, handsome, eyes to kill for. Beneath those Italian designer trousers lurked a magnificent member, whose full, joyous length Loretta took inside her whenever she felt like it. She liked her personal assistants strong on the personal. Sex and power. And money. And sex. It's all there is. Live fast and die young, that was Loretta's motto. She lived fast, and if she hadn't died young yet, she was working on it.

"Yes, Loretta?"

John's honey tones came through the intercom. Loretta thought quickly as she looked at her gold Rolex. She'd wanted to get into the Ferrari and drive to her Long Island mansion, take a jacuzzi and have some sex. But, hell, she could have the sex now.

"Get in here, John. I want you."

Writhing, thrusting passionately on Loretta's desk, their twin bodies pounding, all those hours at the health club coming in very useful. His magnificent member filling her with pleasure, each frenzied thrust lifting them higher, higher, to a plane of esctasy, then on, on into oblivion.

Zack Mariano, frustated, angry. Alone in his loft-studio. The world's most desirable women have been in and out of his bed but Josette bites like a boa-constrictor. In her coils no man escapes. She loves the sex but she loves the power. Sex is good but power gets you to the top, where you get more sex, and power, and money. It's all there is.

"Josette," moans Zack. He's tasted Paradise and wants more. That girl's in his system, like a poison. He can't escape. No man can look upon those firm young breasts, that golden cascade of soft hair, and escape. Zack is her prisoner. Solitary confinement, no remission.

Damn. God damn. Must get her back. Jesus. Need that girl. Gotta have her again. Poison in the system. Like a drug. Addict. Got. He strides to one of the great plate-glass windows that stare out over the urban jungle. Not many loft apartments have got plate-glass windows but Zack's has.

"Where are you, Josette?" he cries, like a man lost.

Somewhere Josette laughs. The fly is in her web.

Loretta in her Ferrari. She loves that car. She likes her cars like her men – fast, gorgeous, powerful, and with full air-conditioning. The Ferrari's engine purrs as she takes it up to 120 on the freeway. The engine throbs, pure Italian power. Slips a tape into the player. Vivaldi. Classical music. Loretta is sophisticated. She has classical records, books.

Because she wants to forget her past.

Twenty-two years earlier. A homeless, starving gypsy woman gives birth to a child under a static caravan in Cromer.

That night the temperature drops to minus 14. The mother dies. The child is left, starving and helpless. It grows up wild, in the grassy flatlands around Great Yarmouth. Lives on worms and berries. Found by a tramp. Bullied, abused, sent to buy Carlsberg Special Brew from Thresher in Lowestoft.

At eight, sent to the poorhouse. Starved, beaten. Stows away on a container ship at Harwich. Arrives in Hamburg, so undernourished she spends three years modelling Sindy clothes in a toy-store. Smuggles herself aboard a 747 bound for New York. A gypsy street-orphan. The shame of her background haunts her still.

Blotted from her mind.

Baron Frederick von Epsenberg. The richest man in the world. Multi-trillionaire. Owns hotels, shipping lines, magazines, TV networks, armaments companies. Houses in 28 countries. Five yachts. Private 747. Own terminal at JFK.

Own terminal heart condition.

The Baron is 87 years old. Two heart attacks in the last year.

Loretta in her jacuzzi, opens *People* magazine. Sees the article. Baron Frederick von Epsenberg wants more than anything to marry again.

Loretta smiles to herself as she reaches for her vibrator.

Josette on assignment. Sandy Lane, Barbados. Playground of the rich, and the even richer. Fat cats with time to kill and jet-skis to ride. Billion-dollar deals are done in scuba-suits.

Josette stretches like a cat on the soft white sands. Her firm young body shines in the sun beneath her Bergasol Factor 8. No man can take his eyes off her. Everywhere, trunks are straining.

She takes out her copy of Boethius' *The Consolation of Philosophy* that she is reading. Josette is a smart girl. She took her degree in Medieval History at Oxford, England; then finishing school in Paris, to learn how to choose curtains. And trap men. Nice girls need rich husbands. And nice curtains. Just 19 years old, but knows just what she wants. She's going to get it. Money, power, sex. And then probably a bit more sex.

Puts down her copy of Boethius, picks up *Hello!*. Eight-page spread on supermodel Barishna Zaphod-Beeblebrox and her 23-bedroom Moorish mansion in Cap d'Antibes.

"Bitch," mutters Josette. Turns the page.

Baron Frederick von Epsenberg wants to marry again.

"Vain old bastard," mutters Josette. "Where can I meet him?"

16

Zack roaming Central Park, lost without Josette. A drug in his veins. Her face etched into his mind. How? How can he get her back, how can he once again stroke those firm young breasts and taste those lips with their promise of paradise that waits, dewy-eyed, between her firm young legs? What had she said? Hardly anything. No words were needed between them. Body language said it all. They had hardly talked, two beautiful people, alone and hot for each other. Besides which, they are both utterly thick and had had nothing to say.

But what was the one thing she had said? Something about wanting to found a magazine empire that would put *Vogue*, *Harpers*, and *Railway Modeller* out of business. Zack smiles to himself. The chick's a smart cookie. She knows what she wants and she knows exactly how she'll get it. She'll use that gorgeous, firm young body if that's what it takes. She had him wriggling like a trout on a hook.

Zack in a phone box. Dials his bank manager.

"How much can I borrow?"

Loretta Platinum writhing on her circular bed, silken sheets smooth beneath her firm young buttocks. Above her Marty Rockman, America's hottest chat-show host, moans his ultimate ecstasy into her ear as his huge, gorgeous cock fills her with shivering pleasures and they enter Love's temple together.

"Again," she whispers, urgently, her insatiable lust roaring like a tigress in the jungle.

"Sure, baby," he moans, his member responding to her caresses, rising proud, standing in tribute to the charms of her gorgeous young body, her firm young breasts with their swollen nipples and the flat firm young stomach with its dewy covering of sweat from the intensity of their passion.

Again they thrash like crazed beasts, urging each other on, until once again they stand at the threshold of Love's temple. Loretta cries out and Marty realises, to his horror, that he's due in the studio in five minutes.

As his Lamborghini streaks off down the driveway Loretta lowers her firm young body into the jacuzzi and thinks about Baron Frederick. Just let me get him to the altar, she thinks. One night with me and he'll suffer the biggest heart attack any multi-trillionaire ever suffered. She thinks of what she could do with the money, and the power. She smiles to herself as she reaches for her vibrator.

Kristeen d'Alivera-Mulova. Half-Czech, half-Spanish and half-Eskimo, her exotic beauty has enticed and captured men all over the world. Fifty years old but with the skin, teeth and hair of an eighteen-year-old. The eighteen-year-old was a High School student who died in a car-crash the previous year. Kristeen paid half a million to the I'Mmoral Clinic in Switzerland for the surgery.

She has no role in this story, but we need to have an older woman who is devastatingly attractive and sexy so that older women can identify with her, so my publishers tell me. Is that okay?

"Josette? Zack."

Zack on his mobile, from his table in Bella's, the most famous restaurant in New York. The place to see and be seen. Paparazzi at the door and Montrachet at the table. Zack says hi to Kevin Costner who's just walked in. The maitre d' brings Zack six oysters.

"Zack? Zack who?"

"Zack. World's hottest fashion photographer. We met on the shoot, a few days back."

Josette sighs. Her sigh comes down the line from her suite at the Bâtard Riche Hotel, Paris.

"Jeez, Zack. It was just a physical thing, just a hump. You're history. I've got to go now. I'm on a shoot."

"Listen to me, baby. You wanted to set up a magazine empire? Well, you've got it, hot chick. I've got the bread."

Josette yawns.

"How much?"

"Just eight million to start with. I've put up my apartment as collateral. You're going to be the hottest glossy-magazine tycoon in the world."

Josette smiles to herself as she puts the phone down and dials Concorde reservations.

Loretta Platinum wrapped her long, tanned legs around Brad Topaz and felt his thick, hard cock thrust deep inside her. Together they panted like crazed beasts until finally they stood at the threshold of Love's temple and then, with the universe exploding in a million shards of crystal dewdrops around them, they sacrificed their passion on Venus' altar and lay together while the warm tide of ecstasy washed over them like a wave.

"Oh, baby, baby," murmured Brad. Brad Topaz, America's hottest TV weatherman, and boy!, Loretta knew every inch of his warm frontal system now.

"Do it to me again," she murmured, pouring a little Moet et Chandon onto his thick, tangled chest hair.

"Sure thing, babe," he murmured. "Let me phone the station. I'm due to give the latest bulletin in half an hour."

"Screw the bulletin!" barks Loretta. "We've got other weathermen, Brad. Let them tell the viewers whether it's gonna rain or not. I want you right here. I need you again!"

With her cherry lips she teases Brad's thick manhood into life once again and again they thrash like rampant beasts on the silk sheets. Loretta claws at the sheets and moans out her pleasure. Soon they stand at the threshold of Love's temple and then, with a shuddering series of frenzied jerks and groans Brad spends inside her, sending her into a whirling vortex of ecstasy. Brad kisses her firm breasts and lies beside her, his chest heaving.

"You're fired, Brad," says Loretta.

"But..."

"No buts. You're history. Adios. I just wanted to have you before you went."

Brad leaves, a broken man. In six months he will be doing the weather for Station NYSK-local cable TV in Raccoon Pelt, Idaho. Loretta doesn't give him a second thought. She is ruthless. She knows what she wants and she'll use any man for her purposes.

She sinks luxuriously into the jacuzzi and smiles to herself as she reaches for her vibrator.

Josette eases her long, tanned legs and her firm young body out of the Porsche 911 parked outside the 32-storey polarized-glass tower of Carrera Magazine Empire Inc., Park Avenue. In just six short months her publishing empire had grown into the biggest international success story the world had ever seen. Already *Vogue* was bankrupt and *Harpers & Queen* in receivership. Josette's glossy fashion mag was selling five million copies a month to the richest and most influential women in the world.

Josette rides the elevator to her penthouse office suite and calls Milan.

"Where are those photos?"

"They are aboard your private jet as we speak."

"Good."

One of her personal assistants, Ramon de Perez-Hectobar, ex-Chippendale and son of a multi-trillioniare Brazilian shipping magnate, brings her a cup of tea.

"Thanks, Ramon. Now get out, you're fired."

Josette is ruthless. She knows what she wants and she'll get it any way she can. She takes her love on the run and casts her men aside like used crisp-bags. But the men come back for more. Bees round the honey pot. Josette can grind her high heels in their faces and still they beg for more. Because she has power, and money. And sex.

19

The Metropolitan Opera, New York. Placido Domingo is to sing *La Bohème* and the crème de la crème of New York society is here.

Josette is in the bar. She is dressed to kill, and over in the corner is her prey. Baron Frederick von Epsenberg adjusts his deaf-aid before going in for the first Act of the opera. Josette moves in for the kill. He gazes at her firm young breasts swelling beneath her Asprey 200-diamond necklace and he is wriggling on her line like a trout.

Loretta Platinum comes out of the Powder Room and sees everything. Josette and the Baron are arm-in-arm. Loretta feels a swelling of rage, and hate. Her bitterness will never end. She vows revenge.

Loretta strides from the building into the fresh air, her mind swirling. All her darkest plans to marry the Baron have been snatched by that scheming little...

Suddenly she is aware of a figure in the street. A tramp, with a beard, dressed in rags, clutching a bottle of Thunderbird and moaning to himself.

For second she thinks she is back in Cromer. She screams.

"Don't scream," says a rasping voice. It is Zack. Reduced to poverty by Josette. She took his money, took his heart and dumped them like garbage, leaving him destitute, without a cent, a broken man. Now he wanders the streets of his broken dreams.

"Don't I know you?" says Loretta.

"I used to be Zack Mariano, hottest fashion photographer in the world, but I gave all my money to Josette Carrera. She used it to found the most fabulously successful magazine empire in the world and then threw me away."

"That's a terrible story," says Loretta, her heart touched.

"It's okay. She threw my heart away long ago. I can't feel anything anymore. Just this emptiness inside. It's like a void. There's nothing."

"I, too, have reason to hate Josette Carrera," breathes Loretta, her voice cracked with emotion. "She has snared the man I wanted, and furthermore, there are rumours in the financial pages of the *New York Times* and other leading newspapers that she plans a takeover bid for the ATC network, thus becoming one of the most powerful media magnates in the world at the age of just twenty."

"Then I guess that fortune has thrown us together, like two corks tossed on the tempestuous seas of fortune."

"Zack, come back to my Park Avenue multiplex and let's make love."

"No, let's not 'make love'. Two torn souls like ours cannot 'make love'. We can only join together like beasts in an animal fury of passion, and then fall back spent onto the satin sheets."

"Ok, let's do that then."

"The bride and groom!"

It is the wedding of the year. Baron Frederick von Epsenberg, the world's richest man, marries Josette Carrera, the richest media tycoon in the world. The reception takes place at Xanadu, Epsenberg's 118-bedroom Long Island mansion. Named after the house in *Citizen Kane*.

Two thousand guests mingle on the lawns. Jack Nicholson chats to Prince Andrew. Adrios Necharchis, the Greek shipping multi-trillionaire, is deep in discussion with Noel Edmonds.

Zack and Loretta have gatecrashed the party. Disguised as waiting-staff, they mingle with caviar and champagne on silver salvers, hunting, hunting their prey.

Josette, in her bridal gown made specially in Paris at a cost of $75,000, is thinking ahead to tonight, when, in the water-bed aboard the Baron's private Boeing, he will experience the joys of her firm young body. It will be his last flight. By the time the plane lands, Josette will be the richest woman on earth.

"More champagne?"

Josette turns and sees the deadly eye of the revolver pointed at her firm young breasts.

"This is to avenge those you have wronged!" cries Loretta, her eyes flashing.

"Yes, it is!" cries Zack, casting aside his waiter's garb and pulling a sub-machine gun from his trousers.

"Who – what – why?"

"I am Zack," cries Zack. "Who you used and abused and tossed aside like a piece of satsuma peel to be tossed aside."

"And I am one who saw my future husband stolen away by your wiles," says Loretta, her flashing eyes spelling danger.

Suddenly another waiter comes forward.

"Wait!" he says. "For am I not a waiter. I am – "

"Father!" cries Josette.

"You know me?"

"Mother left me a note to say that I would recgnize you by the tattoo on your neck. It is as she said – the entwined snakes, and the Harley Davidson logo."

"Secretly I have followed your career all these years," croaks the old man. "But I never made myself known, for I did not want to shame you."

"Stand aside, old man!" cries Loretta, "This bitch must die!"

"No! Do not shoot!"

"Why?"

"Because...because...you two are sisters."

Flashbulbs pop, grown men faint, the *Hello!* reporter develops an erection.

"Sisters? But how can this be after all these years?"

"Yes. Shamefully, your mother and I abandoned both of you – Loretta under a caravan in Cromer, and Josette in Tesco's car-park outside Norwich. But the two of you both grew up, unaware of each other's existence, and both became incredibly beautiful, successful and rich in your own fields. But now, the love of the same man has brought you almost to murder."

"Love? What's love?" cries Josette. "I only want his money."

"So did I," confesses Loretta. "The thought of spending more than one night in the same bed as his wrinkled, gnarled old manhood is unbearable."

"Quick! Come quick!" cries Martin Scorcese. "The Baron has just died!"

"What?" breathes Josette. "Then I am rich!"

"I'm afraid not," says a tall, distinguished-looking man next to her. "For I'm sorry to say that it seems the Baron had been using various fraudulent business practices including insider dealing, junk bonds and creative accounting. It seems that he is worth nothing!"

The party was over. But the two sisters had found each other again. And this time nothing was going to separate them.

Or was it?

"There's just one thing," Loretta said, as they huddled round the brazier with the rest of the down-and-outs. "I thought it said at the beginning of this book that your mother was French and your father was half Puerto-Rican and half-Scottish?"

"That's what I used to tell people to hide my shame," said Josette.

"Oh, good. For a minute, I thought this was one of those books where the author doesn't even bother to correct inconsistencies."

"It is. I was lying."

OTHER BESTSELLING TITLES AVAILABLE:

Sex & Desire & Ambition

Desire & Ambition & Sex

Destiny's Lust

Diamonds & Passion & Destiny

To The Very Top

Hollywood Supermodel

Palm Beach Heiress

No Researcher Necessary

Money For Old Rope

More Money For Old Rope

Destiny's Daughter of Lust

High Heels and Jewellery

Buy Me Everything

Endless Passion & Sex

Designer Labels & Lust

Mini-Series Rights Available

Sex & Desire & Money & Fame

Maximum Money, Minimum Talent

Old & Facelifted & Sad

COOKERY

"Perhaps the best book ever written about cooking with milk."

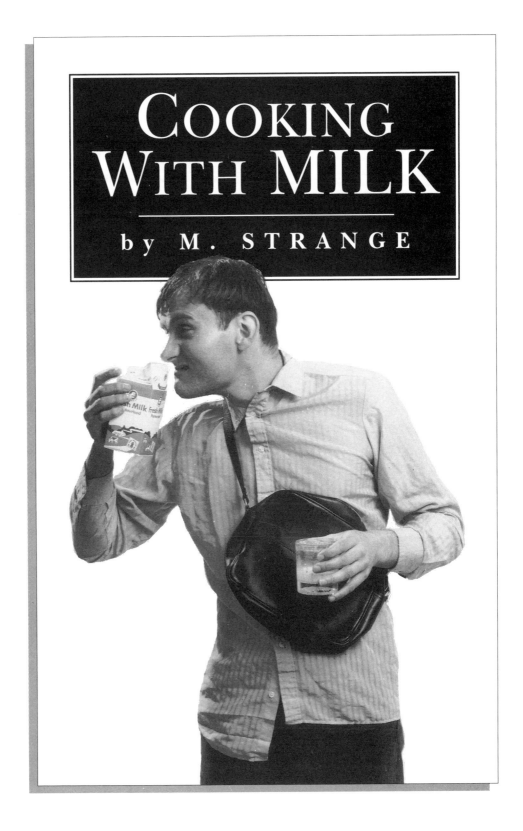

INTRODUCTION

Milk is one of the commonest ingredients in cooking. Indeed there is barely a pudding, sweet or cake that does not require its presence. We drink it in tea, coffee and hot chocolate. We pour it on our breakfast cereal and muesli, and yet there is still far more that can be done with it. There are completely new milks to explore. How many of us have tried camel milk, monkey milk, or the milk of the llama? How many of us have ventured beyond fresh milk to off milk, to lumpy milk, to cheesy green milk with great solid globules in it, milk that takes your head off when you open the carton? The world of milk is vast and is there for us to explore in *Cooking With Milk.*

Milk is nature's food. It has been used since the dawn of time. The Promised Land of the Bible is a land of milk, and honey, and given that they didn't have fridges in Palestine at the time of Herod, that milk must have been pretty warm and lumpy. In Ancient Egypt, Cleopatra bathed in milk. I did that once. The difference was that I didn't get out for three days. And then I *couldn't* get out. I was trapped in half a hundredweight of cheddar. Lovely.

Nowadays milk is generally pasteurised. This is a process named after a French scientist, Louis Pasteur, who devoted his life to making sure that milk was germ-free and hygienic to drink. To many Pasteur is one of the great scientific geniuses of the twentieth century, but to me he is a complete and utter bastard, for killing all the things that I like to see swimming in my milk. Before his process came into universal usage many of the recipes in this book could be made from fresh milk. Now it is necessary to let the milk fester for a few weeks in order to get the same effect.

All the recipes in this book are nutritious and inexpensive to prepare. Preparation time is generally minimal, although if you have a fridge and you are hoping to produce some of the more fragrant dishes within the next six months, it makes sense to switch it off now and move it closer to the stove.

Milk Soup

INGREDIENTS:
Milk

Get some milk and leave it until it's all lumpy. Lovely. Just look at it for a bit, and then sniff it, taking long deep breaths. Then pour it into a saucepan and heat it up. Turn off the gas and leave it. Eat it cold about four days later.

PREPARATION TIME:
The longer the better

Milky Milk in Milk Sauce

INGREDIENTS:
Milk

Take some milk (cartoned) and leave it on the kitchen window sill for a few weeks. Until it feels nice and firm. Lovely.
Take some other milk and put it on your radiator.
If you don't have one, a night-storage heater will do just as well.
Take the first carton, and cut it open with a pair of scissors (rusty if possible).
Remove the carton to leave a solid, rectangular lump of putrid milk. Remove any little worms or weevils that may be living in it, and place on a plate. Take the other milk and pour over. Shake vigorously if it does not emerge initially.
Garnish with the worms and weevils.
This meal is especially tasty if accompanied by a 1969 lemon yoghurt.

PREPARATION TIME:
Three weeks in hot weather, two months in cold.

Milk "de bonne heure"

INGREDIENTS:
Milk

Get a cow. Milk it. Drink the milk. Do not pasteurise.

PREPARATION TIME:
As quick as possible, or the farmer may see you. My brother got shot perfecting this recipe.

Camel Milk "de bonne heure"

INGREDIENTS:
Camel Milk

Get a camel. Milk it. Drink the milk. Call a doctor.

PREPARATION TIME:
Minutes

RECOVERY TIME:
Several months

Llama Milk "de bonne heure"

INGREDIENTS:
Llama Milk

Get a joke. Milk it. Lovely.

Milk "avec fluff de frigidaire"

INGREDIENTS:
Milk
Fluff from under the fridge

"This recipe is one of my favourites. It is quick to prepare and can be very nutritious, depending on what has fallen down the back of the fridge. Normally the fluff will have some peas and some breadcrumbs in it, but if you are lucky, there might be a dead mouse or something."

Take some milk, the lumpier the better. Get a broom and sweep the fluff from under the fridge into a small pile. Dip the lumps of milk in the fluff. Then eat them. Lovely.

PREPARATION TIME:
A couple of weeks' fluff is probably best.

....

Milk "avec fluff de belly button"
(also known as Milk "avec belly bogies")

INGREDIENTS:
Milk
Belly button fluff (blue if possible)

"This is an interesting variation on milk avec fluff de frigidaire, which can be too dry for certain palates. The belly-button fluff, by contrast, is almost always a little sweaty and moist. Unfortunately, if you have an "outy" belly button you will not be able to enjoy this delicacy, unless of course you use someone else's fluff. Which, the more I think about it, sounds quite nice."

Take some milk, the lumpier the better. Lift your anorak and rub the lumps of milk in your belly button until all the fluff has been removed. Take the fluff-rolled lumps and eat, savouring the delicate mixture of milk, fluff, hair, sweat and whatever else you keep in there.

PREPARATION TIME:
Depends on the depth of your navel, or whoever's navel you are using.

29

Milk "avec fromage de knob"

INGREDIENTS:

Milk

Fromage de knob

"This recipe has been deleted by my editor for 'reasons of taste', which is ridiculous. It tastes very nice."

POP BIOGRAPHY

"Cormack's many fans will be fascinated by this meticulously researched book, perhaps the finest music biography since *Renée and Renato: The Severed Alliance.*"

MUSIC
was my first love:
A LIFE OF TIM CORMACK

THIS OLD HOUSE

Dawn breaks over the countryside of Surrey, England, part of the strip of land known as the "green belt" which prevents the British capital from sprawling indefinitely until its suburbs disappear into the Channel. This fragile cocoon of

Marksham Place. One of Cormack's highly trained guard cows has noticed the cameraman

greenery is held together by the M25, an orbital motorway planned in the Sixties, built in the Seventies and repaired in the Eighties by the Department of Transport – a British governmental body whose very existence comes as a surprise to any visitor to the UK.

Marksham Place is a stately manor house nestling in 350 acres of woodland and garden. It is one of the homes of Tim Cormack, who is just waking, on this morning in late spring, lying crossways in his nine-foot-square bed. The French linen sheets are changed daily by one of the team of housekeepers, but already they

are rumpled, fetid, encrusted with stains no forensic scientist would relish examining.

At the foot of the bed, a 24-inch Sony colour television flickers aimlessly. It is wired to a Toshiba twin-load VCR; both remotes are lost under pillows somewhere. The last tape to be played has finished long before. Scattered across the antique Chinese carpet are empty videocassette boxes – *Sunset Boulevard*, *Citizen Kane*, *Casablanca*, *Duck Soup*, *Hot And Willing*, *Ninotchka*, *This Is Spinal Tap*, *Electric Blue 28*.

The heavy, dark curtains are drawn; only fleeting shafts of light poke through to illuminate the collection of rare Victorian prints hung on the walls, which themselves are decorated with hand-printed Colefax and Fowler wallpaper. In one corner stands an enormous Biedermeyer wardrobe, bought at Sotheby's for £55,000. Inside it are empty rows of hooks. Most of Cormack's clothes are abandoned in one corner, next to the Georgian washstand and a small Queen Anne chair. On the wall above the mantelpiece is a large, gilt-edged mirror once owned by the Duke of Wellington. Against the mantel, which is eight feet across, constructed of Dolomite marble with a hearth flagged in reclaimed nineteenth-century tiles, leans a 1957 Fender Stratocaster, bought for £4,500 just a few weeks earlier. Several broken strings lie on the floor; the previous night, Cormack had tried to re-string it after consuming two and a half bottles of Chateau Margaux 1959. Now the empty bottles lie casting a radium-green glow on the floor, along with a half-empty bottle of Librium.

Propped against the wall is a Hokada 12-string, and lying next to it – one of its pick-ups amateurishly unscrewed – is a 1963 Rickenbacker. Cormack bought it after seeing it advertised as "once owned by George Harrison". This turned out to be true: George Harrison had been burgled two days earlier. Cormack also paid £7,300 at auction for a Rickenbacker "once owned by Pete Townshend". After signing the cheque he was given several splinters of wood, some bits of wire and half a scratchplate.

The bedside table is a clutter of matches and ashtrays containing the ash of numerous smokable substances. There are several old newspapers, assorted magazines including an edition of *GQ* with Tim Cormack on the front. A coffee mug, inscribed "B.I.M Records" contains a sludge of three-day-old coffee. A Hitachi radio-alarm shows the time to be 9.35 am.

Tim Cormack is awake. Above the bed is an early Braque, worth about three-quarters of a million. Over the dresser is a tiny framed sketch by Raoul Dufy, and on the opposite wall hangs a framed poster for one of his own shows, at the Epidaurus Amphitheatre on the Peloponnesian peninsula, Greece (the show where he recorded the video *Tim Cormack Live in the Cradle of Western Civilization*).

Cormack doesn't feel too good. He wanders out of the bedroom and into one of the house's seven bathrooms. This one is the biggest: tiled in English porcelain, it contains a large, sunken jacuzzi bath, a multi-jet shower, two sinks set in polished Cornish granite, a sauna and a cold-plunge pool. Cormack cleans his teeth, using an Oral-B medium-bristle brush bought over two years before, and Mentadent Mint. This is his favourite toothpaste, recommended by his personal astrologer, who advised him that Colgate brings ill-fortune to those under the sign of the Bull. In the cabinet to his left is his collection of soaps stolen from hotels around the world. After his previous two tours, it is an extensive collection – 26 Hiltons alone, several hundred in all.

He wanders downstairs, towards the main kitchen. The house is too big for him when he is alone; he feels lost in it. The 18-bedroomed early Victorian mansion confuses him. Outside, to the front, he can see, 100 yards away, the row of trees which hide the ten-foot brick wall enclosing

33

the grounds. The house is on the site of an old manor totally rebuilt in the 1840s. At the top of the drive, parked on the gravel expanse in front of the house, are a Range-Rover, an Aston Martin DB-5, a 1934 Lagonda, a 1957 Porsche 911, and a Unigate milk-float bought for amusement at parties. Beside it sits a Rover 800Si which Cormack uses when wanting to remain anonymous. The Mercedes 450 SL with its TC2 plate is tucked away in the garage, along with the Alfa Spyder, the 1961 Mercedes SL gull-wing, the Pontiac Firebird, the 1950s Alvis, the Ferrari GTO, the "Van den Plas" Austin Allegro 1.3 with a radio aerial made out of a coathanger (from Harrods menswear department), and a Jaguar XJS. Tim Cormack cannot drive, but he enjoys looking at his cars, and his accountants and investment advisors will frequently remove them for long periods for "mechanical checks and valuations". There is also a 1966 Mini-Cooper and an early Ford Zodiac, as well as the bikes – a Kawasaki 1100, a Harley Davidson Electra Glide, two 900cc BMWs, an old Triumph RAF bike, and a rally-specification Kawasaki 250, which Tim likes to ride around the grounds. Parked around the back of the house is a Hawker Hurricane. Cormack doesn't really know what to do with it: he'd wanted a Spitfire but none were available; he can't fly, and is too

apprehensive to learn, so the Hurricane sits on the lawn next to the Boeing 737 (an unwanted gift) and a Sea King helicopter which Cormack has had painted white and which he uses as a greenhouse.

Once in the kitchen, Tim is even more lost. Quite at home in a digital recording studio, adept at programming a Synclavier or operating a 48-track computer-controlled recording console, he has yet to work out how to operate the Aga which the designer thoughtfully installed in his kitchen. The conventional cooker – a Guggenau in brushed aluminium – is easier to handle. A full-size Gaggia cappuccino/expresso maker sits on the worktop. Tim removes a jar of Nescafé from one of the hand-built English oak cabinets and makes his way over to the sink. The floor, laid with African slate tiles, looks beautiful but is rather cold when you've lost your slippers. Bathed in the light from the sixteen recessed halogen spots in the ceiling, Tim sits down at the breakfast bar to eat a bowl of Rice Krispies, taking a carton of semi-skimmed milk from the six-foot-high 1955 Westinghouse fridge. His personal nutritionist, Nathan P. Fraud Jnr., has devised a ten-day-cycle food regimen which allows Tim a bowl of Rice Krispies a day. It also allows him unlimited amounts of fruit pastilles, Kronenbourg 1664, french fries in white bread (the English call this a "chip butty") and anything else Tim likes to eat. Basically, for £1200 a consultation, Nathan will allow his clients to eat whatever they want.

In another corner of the room sits a 1960s Wurlitzer jukebox, stocked with classic Motown, Stax, early Beatles and a couple of oddities from Tim's own collection, including Pinky and Perky (a British puppet-pig duo) singing "The Pushbike Song" and a flexidisc about investment opportunities with Cedar Holdings, which fell out of a copy of a magazine when Tim was a child.

Cormack's personal chef, Gaspard de Renaud, has been at work since 5.30 am, when he drives from the markets in London down to Marksham Place. Together with his team of two sous-chefs, he will produce four slices of toast for Tim to eat around 9.30. Cormack always spreads this with Golden Shred marmalade. His previous cook, Graham le Marron, was sacked after purchasing Sainsbury's own-brand maramalade by mistake. Marron returned to the kitchen of the George V in Paris, while Cormack, badly shaken, went into three months of intensive psychotherapy to get over "routine-interruption shock syndrome". Later, the incident stimulated a creative outburst and a batch of songs including "Get the Spread Right" and the American No. 1, "Wrong Marmalade, Wrong Job",

described by *Rolling Stone* as "an anthem for incredibly spoiled rich idiots everywhere".

Tim Cormack is in his 33rd year. He looks youthful but, close-up, his face bears the lines of many late nights and exhausting days travelling. His features are well-known; his hair untidy. His Surrey home is one of nine; he also owns an old baronial hall in Scotland and a minor chateau in the Loire valley in France, keeps an apartment on Park Avenue South in New York, an old plantation house in Barbados, an apartment in Berlin, a house in the 14th arrondissement in Paris, a 28-floor split-level penthouse in Tokyo, and a static caravan in Cromer. His accountants have also bought him a hotel in Ireland, but forgot to tell him.

It is a Tuesday morning, and he has little to do. Not due to tour for another couple of months, he will not begin rehearsal until two weeks before. His last album, *Hoo-Hah*, was released six months ago; it is currently at No. 4 in the British album chart. He is currently in a major legal wrangle with his American record company, Globahype, over his contract. The wrangle is complex: Cormack wants a clause guaranteeing "total artistic and creative freedom" while Globahype are insisting on a clause guaranteeing "the right to

Douglas Liddle, Head of Marketing at Globahype MegaCorps – "I know what the kids on the street are into. We must acquire more rap-boogie hippety-hop grunge-swing product"

make sure everything on this album sounds exactly like everything on the last album". The initial mixes of the songs for Cormack's new album, *Millions Starve and Die*, have met with an unenthusiastic response from Globahype executives, who are worried that the album does not contain a hit single to match "Kick It Down the Stairs" on *Hoo-Hah*.

At the moment, Cormack is insisting that the first release from *Millions Starve and Die* is the six-minute track "Chernobyl Foetus".

Tim's only appointment today is to expect a phone call around lunchtime concerning a request to appear at a charity show for Amnesty International, possibly to play guitar while John Cleese sings "My Way".

chapter 2

BORN TO BOOGIE

Tim Cormack was born on March 5th 1960. When the Beatles cut their first disc, he was just two years old, but his mother clearly remembers him listening to "Love Me Do" on the radio and uttering his first words: "No way is Ringo playing those drums."

His musical abilities were precocious. His mother, Myra Cormack, had a piano which had been left to her by her great-aunt. She did not play it, but used it as a nesting-place for her collection of pet hamsters. The young Tim threw all the hamsters out and began to teach himself to play. In many ways, he displayed uncanny similarities to the young Mozart — an instinctive grasp of harmony; the ability to play something perfectly by ear after just one hearing; and a penchant for wearing white periwigs with a bow on the back.

In early 1961, with young Tim just under a year old, Myra's husband Graham left her for an assistant in the local hardware shop, leaving her alone with her six offspring. Taking to drink, she spent most of her time in the local pub, the Cheese and Whippet, where she met Tim's future stepfather Norman, a debt-collector and small-time crook who hated children, especially ones who displayed any musical ability. Norman forced Tim to crouch for hours to provide a foot-rest while he watched television, frequently complaining about the sex and violence and how there wasn't nearly enough of it. For over a year, Tim was forced to sweep chimneys 18 hours a day, and was frequently locked in his bedroom with only a trained rat for company. In November 1963, President Kennedy was assassinated in Dallas, Texas, and the whole world mourned the loss of this charismatic young leader – apart from Norman, who felt Kennedy was a "poof".

As Tim got older, he outgrew his leg-irons and Norman was forced to set him free occasionally. Norman and Myra fought frequently, often using three of the children as judges. One evening in 1965, after Tim's mother had controversially won on points after a 12-round bout, Norman became incensed and burnt the house down. For six months the family roamed around the country, homeless and starving, suffering from malnutrition, disease and losing touch completely with current fashion trends. Two of Tim's brothers were torn to pieces by stray dogs and his sister Dana was run over by a train after drinking too much gin. Tim was to use his memories of this period in his early song, "Shit Childhood".

Critics have long been divided over the influence of Tim's early years on his work. The Canadian rock writer John Strazzle has always felt that, "the shadow of Tim's stepfather falls across all Cormack's work," citing as examples songs like "Horrible Stepfather". Cormack himself has always denied any obvious link between his life and his work, but as British critic Annie Binch put it, "That's crap".

While Cormack was fighting off infection and struggling to survive as a down-and-out with his alcoholic mother and violent stepfather, the British pop scene was exploding. The Merseybeat boom had crossed the Atlantic, the Beatles were playing Shea Stadium and in San Francisco the psychedelic movement was just beginning to mushroom. Groups like the Barry Topkinson Experience, the Spencer Franks Group and the Four Dullards were hitting the charts. Tim Cormack, at five years old, heard the Rolling Stones' "Little Red Rooster" and commented to his mother that the fusion of the Chicago Blues style with mainstream British pop was producing interesting results.

"...a man ahead of his time." Cormack's punk period began in 1964

Eventually Norman died when he accidentally walked in front of a bus in an attempt to pick a halfpenny out of a gutter. Myra took a job sewing novelty bra-and-panties kitchen aprons together for 6d. per 22-hour day, and the family moved into a one-bedroomed flat in South London. Tim now went to school for the first time in his life. Unable to afford the uniform, his mother sellotaped a tie-shaped piece of paper to his shirt every day. Tim

37

swiftly became known as "Stinky Cormack" since the family home had no running water. Swiftly, however, he began to show extraordinary ability in art and music. The school music room was sadly ill-equipped, containing nothing but a xylophone with only three notes on it. At the age of eight, Cormack composed his *Concerto For Xylophone With Only Three Notes On It*. His school report for the year 1969 reads, "Tim is a smelly oik whose musical ability may, one day, prove to be his path out of the gutter." This extraordinarily premonitory comment came from his head-teacher, Mr Jeffrey, who subsequently served five years in Dartmoor for taking showers with the school football team.

chapter 3

SMELLS LIKE TEEN SPIRIT

The British school system went comprehensive in the early 1970s, and, without that change, it is doubtful whether Tim Cormack would ever have met Charles Dunmow. Charles' background was very different to Tim's: his father occupied a senior position in a medium-sized road-haulage company, while his mother was a prominent local figure, church-warden, charity-committee organizer and general middle-class pain. The two boys met, aged 11, in class 1C at Fieldstone School. No-one seems to remember them being particular friends until a few years later, when both developed a keen interest in music, visiting record shops and music shops together. By the age of fifteen they were both, like thousands of other teenagers, engrossed in the music of the time. God knows why – most of it was rubbish.

Classmates remember that Dunmow, at the time, was the more enthusiastic of the two. A slightly gawky fifteen-year old, Dunmow was a fan of the type of "progressive" popular music which went out of fashion in the late 1970s. One contemporary remembers Dunmow as "wearing a large green Yes badge on his lapel and spending most breaktimes trying to convince the rest of his classmates that *Tales From Topographic Oceans* was not complete shit." (Yes were a popular "progressive" band fronted by Jon Anderson who wrote extremely long and complex songs, often with cosmic titles.)

It was at around this age that Dunmow purchased an electric guitar. His father sliced it up with a saw, burnt it in the garden incinerator, and proceeded to call in the local vicar, the Rev. John Samwise, to exorcize Charles' stereo, which, he said, was "possessed by the devil's music". Dunmow worked four paper-rounds and bought another electric guitar, which his father smashed to pieces with a pickaxe. His third electric guitar was found seething gently in a bath of nitric acid, while the fourth was fed to a goat.

Dunmow asked Tim Cormack if he wanted to form a group. Cormack offered to play the bass, and purchased a Woolworths Audition bass guitar. Unable to afford an amplifier, he played through Charles Dunmow's 15-watt Wem amplifier. When the two of them hit a note simultaneously, Dunmow's guitar would become inaudible. Cormack swiftly picked up the rudiments of bass guitar technique; after a few days he was able to follow the root notes of a chord progression by ear. After a few weeks he was accompanying Dunmow on a number of songs it had taken the latter six months to piece together. Dunmow, by all accounts, knew four chords at this time – "C, A, E and four-string D". His ambition was always ahead of his ability. He talked about the musical use of the augmented ninth flat fifth when he had trouble mastering the F major bar-chord.

Tim's own musical output seems to have been faltering during this period. In his mid-teens, Cormack was dissatisfied and bored with current chart pop. The last straw appears to have been when he saw Sailor singing

"Girls Girls Girls" on *Top of the Pops*. He didn't enjoy school, and felt he was going nowhere.

Meanwhile, in the clubs of New York, the New York Dolls, Iggy Pop and James Williamson, and Television were the cutting edge of a new style and a new attitude. The underground

Tim's first band. Their first and only single was a Cormack composition, "We're Going To Be So Embarrassed By This When We Get Older." It reached number 134 in Paraguay

movement known as "punk" finally surfaced in Britain on that notorious night in late 1976, when the Sex Pistols were interviewed on live television by Terry Wogan. The exchange that followed has now become pop history:

WOGAN   Johnny Rotten, your new single has divided the critics, hasn't it?

ROTTEN   No, it hasn't. They're unanimous. They hate it.

WOGAN   (LAUGHS) Well, I liked it.

ROTTEN   You've never listened to it.

WOGAN   (LAUGHS) Nay, nay – such scepticism, and from one so young!

39

(LOOKS AT CAMERA AND MAKES FACE) I've listened to it, every second of it, and enjoyed it, every last bit.

ROTTEN   You never bloody have.

WOGAN   (LOOKS AT CAMERA AND SHAKES HEAD) They never believe me. Never! But, gentle viewers, pray list unto me, I have heard it. Now, to move on...

ROTTEN   You dirty rotter.

WOGAN   What was that? (TURNS TO CAMERA AND GRINS) The ol' lugholes, the old Woge's lugholes, are not what they were. Pray, repeat.

ROTTEN   You fucking rotter.

WOGAN   So – tell us about the tour.

SID VICIOUS   You dirty fucking old man.

WOGAN   Fascinating. And will there be hi-jinks on the old tour bus?

ROTTEN & VICIOUS   Fuck off, you fucker!

WOGAN   Well, well, well – fancy that, eh, viewers? What a shame that I'm gettin' too old for that sort of lark.

ROTTEN   This is no fun at all. Can't we have Bill Grundy instead?

Over 1000 calls of complaint were received, and Terry Wogan was suddenly on the front page of every newspaper in the country, with headlines such as SHOULD OUR KIDS BE WATCHING THIS MAN? Cormack, watching at his home in Croydon, was thrilled. The attitude and style of the Pistols was unlike anything he had ever seen. He became a fan overnight.

Dunmow, however, was still influenced by the then-fashionable "progressive" style, writing tunes with titles like "Leylines to Valhalla", "The Rime of the Ancient Mariner", and "The Runestone of Narnia". Then, one day, Dunmow too abruptly switched allegiance.

"One morning, he just turned up with his hair cropped," remembers a classmate. "When I asked him why, he said – 'Fuck off. Questions are the manacles of the system.' I didn't understand this, so I told him he'd be late for maths."

That breaktime, Dunmow had replaced his Yes badge with one that read "Fuck the Police" (the law-and-order organization rather than the music group fronted by Sting). He now started writing in the social-realist style of punk. One day he came in with a song called "Pig Roast":

The Law the forces of repression
The filth arrive in quick succession
Pig Roast! Burn the coppers
Pig Roast! Don't try to stop us

Quite what experience had prompted this invective is uncertain, although Dunmow was once stopped by a policeman for riding a bicycle without a rear light. Another song he wrote at this time was called "Council Estate":

Council estate! Council estate!
Puke and blood and rubbish
* and hate*
Council estate! Council estate!
In adversity they say "hello mate"

This paean to working-class solidarity failed to convince Tim, who pointed out that its author lived in a four-bedroomed detached house, with a mother who had a "Maggie Not Ted" mug in her kitchen.

This led to an argument with Charles, Cormack's musical associate and fellow-songwriter. Cormack favoured "quitting the fascist sausage-factory to oblivion society calls 'school'," and becoming a full-time musician. Charles favoured this too, but said he felt that his O-levels would suffer badly. Cormack gave him a straight choice: leave, and join him on the road to stardom, or stay at school. Dunmow consulted his parents, who informed him that if he left school, they would remove his testes with a Black'n'Decker Strimmer. Furthermore, his father informed him that Tim Cormack was a "degenerate disgrace to the school" who would "end up in the gutter where he belongs". Dunmow sold his guitar and left the group.

Cormack left home, and squatted in a damp flat in Bohemia Street, Notting Hill, an area of West London once torn by racial riots and now a gentrified upmarket area beloved of media types. The flat became a favoured hang-out for musicians, artists, punks, dossers, tramps and hangers-on of every description. One regular visitor was Spit Heroin, guitarist with punk band Aborted Abortion (Heroin's real name was Arthur Fffitch-Glanville). The band's drummer, Phyllis Tyne, was born the Duchess of Herefordshire but dropped out of Roedean at the age of 14 because, in her own words, she "wanted to get off the conveyor-belt to oppression".

Tim auditions for "New Faces", 1971. He was told to "piss off".

Tim went to the premiere of Derek Jarman's *Jubilee*, but got there too late and was refused entry. He went to the Lyceum to see XTC supporting Talking Heads. Unfortunately, it was sold out, and he couldn't get in.

His own band, TCB, were slowly making their name on the live circuit, partly due to the incontinence of the bassist, Graham Boon. Graham was very nervous about going on-stage in front of the public, partly because he was naturally shy, and partly because he was wanted by three different police forces for drug-dealing. This caused him to wet

41

himself with fear at almost every gig, which gave the band a solid reputation as the only band whose bassist regularly wet himself. One night, at the Smeg Club in Balham, in the audience was Ned Jersey, A&R man at Gob Records, the hastily formed punk label of Globahype Corporation. Jersey's brief was to look out for "raw new street talent with attitude and edge". When he saw TCB, he was electrified. "Cormack was playing like a man demented," he recalls. "He had a beaten-up Telecaster round his neck, and when he came to the microphone he sang in a series of strange, staccato noises and would jerk insanely backwards and forwards. I asked him afterwards if he based this style on David Byrne. He told me no, it was just that the microphone was not earthed properly and had 300 volts going through it."

Whatever the origin of Tim's vocal style at this period, TCB were becoming a popular live attraction, for reasons other than the bassist's entertaining incontinence. Their regular following consisted of a cross-section of punks, skinheads, students and commuters. Their appeal to commuters remains a mystery, but Cormack well remembers how their gigs would regularly attract office-workers on their way home. "They would pop to the pub for a drink after work," he recalls, "and then pop in to one of the rock clubs, catch a new band, and then go home to Dorking." Fights were frequent among the commuting element. Their favoured style of dress –

The early TCB auditioning singers, 1975

grey Hornes suit, M&S tie and a pair of nice shoes from Dolcis – marked them out. The punks frequently endured the taunts of the commuter crowd, whose violent tendencies, exacerbated by long waits for trains and lack of seats, made them turn ugly at the slightest provocation. A number of bands who attracted hard-core commuters put adverts in the music press distancing them-selves from them, but Tim never discouraged them, braving the flying umbrellas and copies of the *Standard* that were invariably thrown at the stage.

Inspiration, however, was lacking. The hardcore commuter fans tended to disdain new music, preferring well-established chart hits. In an era when Siouxsie and the Banshees, Magazine, the Cure, the Slits, and the Buzzcocks were redefining British pop, the Tim Cormack Band's most popular songs were their cover of "Oh Lori" by the Alessi Brothers, and their instrumental version of the Rubettes' "Sugar Baby Love". "We're trapped by our fans," Cormack told *Sounds*. "They're great, obviously, but they are shit and know nothing about anything and haven't got the first clue what's good, or bad, or indifferent. They are mostly human vegetables who wouldn't know exciting music if it shat on their heads."

chapter 4

BIKE RIDE TO THE MOON

A leak developed in the roof of the flat and Cormack promptly contacted his Landlord, Mr Ron Villain. Mr Villain pointed to a clause in the rental agreement which stated that, "The Landlord shall undertake to pay for all maintenance work to the Property, EXCEPT THAT in the event that the property actually requires maintenance work, the Landlord shall totally ignore this clause." This is totally standard in Landlord-Tenant agreements everywhere and, finding that there was no prospect of getting Mr Villain to do anything about the leaking roof, and totally unable to afford to pay a builder himself, Tim purchased a second-hand copy of a book that was to change his life – *The Reader's Digest Book of Home Improvement*.

"Suddenly, it was as if all those pent-up creative juices were released," recalled Viv LaFrance, who was squatting in Bohemia Street while trying to secure a recording deal for her band, the Sodden Tampons (they were eventually signed to Spack Records. After three years without any radio airplay, they changed their name to the Sexy Girlies and released "Boys Make My Heart Go Bingy-Bong", which spent six weeks at No. 1). Meanwhile, Cormack had found inspiration.

Within a week, he had recorded rough demos of five new songs on his Portastudio. The first track, "Always Use a Primer", was a straightforward song about painting, but it was the second track, "Paint Your Love on Me (in Two Coats)" which really stood out. The chorus came to Cormack late one afternoon: "Paint your love on me – sha na na na na." Inspiration continued through "You Sand Me Down" – *Melody Maker* described it as a "telling metaphor; that the love of a partner can smooth the edges of a rough personality, and turn it into something smooth and less likely to give you splinters", although the *NME* said it was "simply wooden".

For the sinuous funk of "Building My Patio", Cormack approached Sly and Robbie to produce, but they were out when he phoned. Cormack admired the Shriekback track, "My Spine is the Bassline", and wanted the same feel to the track, or as he said to producer Clarke Crump, "Can we rip that off?"

The success of the record was due in no small part to the efforts of Cormack's new manager, Wes Wade, affectionately known in the business as "Mr Shithead". Wes was a hard negotiator who had little time for charm. Another of his acts, The Bottomleys, had recently left his agency after a dispute over unpaid royalties. Within a year the drummer, bass-player and saxophonist had all been involved in mysterious car crashes. Wes also managed a boxer, two wrestlers, a top international assassin and a Middle-Eastern terrorist group.

Cormack's manager Wes after his conviction for 42,633 counts of fraud, false accounting and withholding of royalties. Cormack described him as "a shark, but a shark in a poolful of piranhas". He still retains Tim's trust, not to mention most of his earnings

ME AND YOU AND A DOG NAMED BOO

Tim Cormack's house looks like a photograph from the opening pages of *Country Life* magazine, which isn't surprising, since that is where he first laid eyes on it. As a teenager he had occasionally flipped through back copies while in dentists' or doctors' waiting-rooms, and had reeled at the sums of money demanded for these vast, gorgeous residences, with their huge acreages of grounds, their outbuildings, cottages, paddocks and pools. By the time he reached his mid-twenties he was in a position to buy one of them, and whiled away long stretches of time on the tour-bus looking through the property pages of the latest *Country Life*.

"What d'you think of this one?" he would ask Wes, showing him a picture of a huge Victorian mansion somewhere in Gloucestershire.

"Naaah," Wes would say. "Looks 'orrible. And no pool."

"I could get one built."

"Bollocks. You don't have to go through all that palaver. Buy a house with a pool already in it."

Tim would flip over the page and find another property, this time a castellated baronial manor in Scotland with a four-figure acreage, a loch, a forest, its own coastline, salmon farm and grouse shoot.

"What about this?"

"Got a pool?"

"Outdoor."

"Bollocks!" Wes would scream. "An outdoor pool in bloody Scotland? You're joking. You'd freeze your knackers off every time you went for a bleeding dip. You'd do your next album sounding like a bleeding castrato."

"What about this then?" Tim would ask, pointing at a picture of a vast Georgian house somewhere in Berkshire.

"Looks alright. Pool?"

"Indoor. And gym, croquet lawn."

"Bollocks to the bloody croquet lawn. How big's the pool?"

"Doesn't say."

"Find out. Anything less than twenty metres isn't worth having. You dive in and smash your bloody skull on the other end. It's crap."

"You're not wrong."

And so the conversation would continue, up and down the motorways of Britain, and up and down the autoroutes, autobahns and autostradas of Europe. I know I wasn't actually there, but most biographies seem to put imaginary conversations in reported speech, so why shouldn't I?

Wherever Tim Cormack

45

toured, his copies of *Country Life* went with him. On countless aeroplane flights, while the rest of the band and crew dozed, drank, ogled the cabin staff or flipped through *High Life*, Tim and Wes would be side by side, talking property.

"Look at this one," says Tim, perhaps."Converted oasthouse in Kent. It's really big and it's got that sort of tower thing on it. Sort of unusual."

"You don't want to live in a bloody oasthouse," replies Wes. "What's an oasthouse anyway?"

"Don't know," admits Tim. "Didn't they store hops in it or something?"

"Why isn't it called a hophouse then? I mean, what's a fucking oast when it's at home?"

Tim thinks about this, and comes up with a suggestion. "It's an anagram of oats."

"So bleeding what? Here, this bloody British Airways coffee is crap, isn't it? Anyway, you don't want to live in Kent."

"Why not?"

"It's bloody boring, that's why not. It's all flat and full of commuters and Home Counties bastards with Vauxhall Novas and bloody stone-clad houses with satellite dishes on."

"That's not Kent," says Tim, in my imagination. "That's Essex."

This kind of banter between artist and manager would go on for hour after hour, and was probably very close to the banter that I've invented above, and tried to pass off as genuine.

After the rigours of the 18-month Home Improvement tour, Cormack bought three houses and worked feverishly on his next project, this time inspired by *The AA Book of Car Maintenance*.

Lochietrossan Hall, Cormack's retreat in Scotland. He goes there six Fridays a year, "to watch 'Absolutely' in the right atmosphere"

chapter 6

ROCK 'N' ROLL SUICIDE

Point Seven Studios, London W8, lie in the basement of a converted stucco-fronted Victorian terraced mansion. From the outside, this imposing building – so typical of the area – bears no sign of the twentieth century, let alone of the state-of-the-art recording facility lurking in the basement.

It was here, during that long, hot summer, that Cormack recorded *Full Service*, the album which was to sell 12 million copies and seal his reputation as one of the world's greatest songwriters and performers. Over four months – a comparatively rapid process in comparison with, say, Tears For Fears – the nine tracks which have pumped ceaselessly from TVs, radios, stereos and shops ever since, were laid down on digital disks.

The sessions were not trouble-free. Tim's self-confidence had grown to a point where, on some songs, he would no longer allow the other members of his band to play the parts they had played in rehearsal. Drummer Harkum was irked to find himself merely adding fills to drum-machine tracks, and for "Signs of Trouble", three days spent EQ-ing and balancing the live drum kit proved to have been utterly pointless when, in the mix, Cormack individually re-dubbed every drum with a sampled sound, including the noise of him hitting the side of a carton of Libby's orange juice with a spoon. ("Signs of Trouble" later won a Grammy for Production.)

Producer Clarke Crump was also alarmed to notice the deterioration in Cormack's health during the recording of the album. His lifestyle was not one calculated to produce maximum fitness. Typically beginning recording in the early afternoon, around two, he would work through solidly for twelve or so hours, leaving at two am and usually heading for one of several clubs – Maja's, Queeg, Limp – where he would remain until around five, heading back to his rented apartment in Notting Hill Gate. It was on one of these night-time sojourns that he met Toni Max, a half-French, half-English model whose mother, Lady Marjorie Hetherington, had died in a head-on collision on the M4 while changing a cassette in her Range-Rover, and whose father was in prison in France for drug-smuggling. Renowned for her voracious appetite for men, she had once been featured heavily in the British tabloids for entertaining a prominent pillar of the banking community in her boudoir a quite unfeasible number of times in one night. She fiercely denied all such stories as "tabloid rubbish", laughing off another which involved a prominent British royal and a moving horse-box. She was, she claimed, trying to start a family, and as soon as possible.

One night, she and Cormack made love for five hours, with the aid of large amounts of cocaine and amyl nitrite; Cormack was still insensible when the entire London Philharmonic Orchestra under Sir Sacheverell Minolti, with Annette Huberduber as violin soloist, assembled in Point Seven's sizeable Live Room waiting to record the orchestral parts for "Windscream Wiper". A phone call to Bohemia Street at 3.45 failed to rouse him from his post-coital stupor and tens of thousands of pounds were wasted. When Derek Menzies, Cormack's A&R contact at Gob Records, tried to chide him for this, Cormack told him, "You're worried? I've got a sore knob."

On other occasions, Toni and Tim simply disappeared for days on end – once to Paris, once to New York, once to the Carribean, where they stayed on a yacht belonging to the chairman of the American promotion company C.I. Showtime. Bass player Wayne Clement accused Cormack at one point of being "too shagged to play", an accusation he never denied, preferring to up his intake of cocaine and, frequently,

amphetamine stimulants to sustain him through the sessions and on to the clubs where, abetted by large quantities of Ecstasy, he would remain all night. Cormack's love-life was the subject of many tabloid columns throughout that summer; as recording proceeded, his name was linked to several actresses, a percussionist, two Roedean sixth-formers, a junior government spokesman on European Affairs, and a children's TV presenter.

Clarke also worried about Cormack's consumption of alcohol during this period; it seemed to be escalating at an alarming rate. Always a bizarre mixer of tastes, Cormack would think nothing of ordering several large takeout pizzas to be delivered to the studio from the local Perfect Pizza, and then eating them ac- companied by a Chateau Lafitte '66, or a bottle of Meursault (for the seafood special). This, along with his crates of specially imported Paraguayan beer, provided a continuous intake of alcohol which, coupled with the occasional tabs of acid, accounts for many of the lyrical oddities on the album. Once, very drunk, Cormack disappeared to visit a local prostitute to "try something Toni won't do". No-one at the studio could begin to guess what on earth this might be. The prostitute performed the act, but unfortunately the money was wasted; Cormack was so stoned at the time that he later reported that he had been "blown by a large fruitbat", and fretted for days about the need for a rabies injection.

One night, high on a cocktail of LSD, cannabis, cocktails and two large deep-pan pizzas, Cormack attacked bassist Wayne Clement with a Gibson SG. Clement parried with an Aria Pro II bass, whereupon Cormack hurled a Yamaha DX7 keyboard across the studio. Missing its target, the airborne synthesiser smashed through the plate-glass window which separated the live area from the control room, landing on the custom-built Technics 48-track digital mixing desk, causing £200,000 of damage and several stitches to be needed in Clarke's face. As the dust settled, "Cormack, with a crazed look in his eye, seized a Fender Telecaster which was sitting in a corner and im-provised the solo to 'Loosen Up' on the spot. It was incred-ible, because the guitar was totally out-of-tune, but this incredible solo flowed out – electric, raw, brilliant."

The studio was awed. Clement, wiping the blood from his nose, could only clap Cormack on the shoulder.

"Fuckin' brilliant," he said. Cormack fell into the eight-piece Sonor drum kit, slashing his forearm on the edge of a Paiste 14" cymbal. Rushed to hospital, he received 20 stitches. Meeting his manager, Crump (who had been sitting at the mixing desk when the keyboard landed on it), in the casualty ward, Cormack totally failed to remember that it was he who had put him there; in fact, he failed to remember his producer at all, mistaking him for Geoff Hurst, scorer of three goals in England's 1966 World Cup soccer final. Since Cormack was only a child at the time, this was a remarkable feat of memory. But no sooner had Crump remarked on this than Cormack was gone. He spent the night at L'Aurore, a club in Brixton, an area of south London once torn by racial rioting but now a gentrified upmarket area beloved of media types.

Cormack's addiction to cocaine in the early 80's ended after seeing this photo-enlargement, showing the inside of his left nostril

PLEASE PLEASE PLEASE PLEASE LET ME GET WHAT I WANT

The album's success made Cormack rich beyond calculation, and it was after a feature in the *Sunday Times* described Cormack as "the most brilliant, original and stinking rich person in the world," that Charles Dunmow's father, Reginald Dunmow, was found hacked to pieces by a madman. A copy of the Cormack article was pinned to the body, with the words "Thanks a lot, Dad" written on it in biro. The culprit was never found. Police interrogated Charles Dunmow, but he was quite happily working in double-glazing telesales, and professed himself "absolutely mystified".

In November 1984, Cormack took a telephone call from Bob Geldof of the Boomtown Rats. Geldof explained to him that he was trying to get together a group of people to record a charity single to raise money for the starving peoples of Africa. Already Bono, George Michael, Paul Young, Simon le Bon and Bananarama had agreed to do it. Cormack told Geldof it sounded like "a daft idea" and rang off.

After "Do They Know It's Christmas?" had become a vast hit, reflecting well on everyone who had participated in its making, plans were hurriedly laid for Cormack to perform at the Wembley Live Aid concert, then go by helicopter to Heathrow and thence by Concorde to Philadelphia, where he would arrive in time to duet with Madonna on "Holiday". Then he would fly back to Wembley on Concorde in order to play guitar for David Bowie, and then back to Philadelphia to play saxophone for Tina Turner. After this, he would fly back to Wembley to sing backing vocals for Elton John and then back to Philadelphia to do the guitar solo on "Stairway to Heaven". After jetting back for the Wembley finale, he would return to Philadephia to join Bob Dylan on stage and try to help him sound slightly less rubbish.

In the event, the schedule proved too complicated, and negotiations broke down over Cormack's demand that the event be titled "Live Aid starring Tim Cormack". The event went ahead with Phil Collins making the transatlantic trip, and Bob Dylan duly sounded rubbish.

In October of 1985 Cormack released his first and only flop, the ill-fated *Tomorrow's World* album. Cormack claimed subsequently that critics misunderstood the record: the title had led to expectations that its theme would be the future of humanity, whereas in fact it was a tribute to a long-running British television series devoted to advances in science. Reviewers unanimously felt that this restrictive subject matter limited the album's appeal. "I've always felt," Cormack told *Railway Modeller*, "that the greatest art goes from the specific to the general, and that a small subject can become magnified metaphorically," but none of this seemed to make any difference. "This self-indulgent paean to a favourite TV show is a total waste of time and money," fulminated Jeff Graham in *Record Mirror*, while the London *Times* felt the record "sadly lacking in absolutely everything". The single from the album, "Judith Hann", only reached number 83 in the chart, and the follow up, "Get Out Your Pointer, William Woollard", did even worse. Listened to today, the album sounds better than it was ever given credit for at the time – the slow, menacing funk of "Another Item About Electric Cars" is particularly effective – but overall, it has to be said, the album is pretty shit, really.

Cormack took the album's failure badly. On 13th November,

he was due to appear on *Wogan*, but became very drunk and abusive in the hospitality room and tried to attack another guest, a man who had cycled across the Himalayas on a Raleigh Chopper to raise money for the mentally handicapped (in the event, most of the money was given straight back to him). The producers held a hurried conference to decide whether Cormack was in any fit state to appear. By the time the discussion was finished, Tim had found his way onto the set anyway. He used foul language, uttered violent threats against Terry Wogan, vomited on the other guests, and punched out a cameraman who refused to sell him any dope. Finally, he passed out unconscious, clutching at Terry as he fell and dragging his toupee off in the process. The press were outraged. Next day, editorials described him as a disgrace, a foul philistine, and an evil influence on the nation's children. The following week every one of his albums was back in the Top Ten, and they stayed there for six months.

c h a p t e r 8

YOU CAN'T ALWAYS GET WHAT YOU WANT

It was after this episode that Cormack became interested in saving the Brazilian rainforests,

joining the Rock Against Logging Project. In 1986 he released the single "Don't Chop Down the Rainforest". By 1987, frustrated at seeing no reduction in logging and no prospect of the Project succeeding, he wrote the song "All Brazilians Are Bastards". The day after the song reached No. 1 around the world, he remembered that he was due to play an open-air concert in Rio de Janeiro the following week.

It was too late to do anything about it. He issued a press statement in which he explained that, "it was perfectly fair that Brazil should exploit its natural resources as all the hypocritical Western nations had already exploited theirs, and that if the world heats up and runs out of oxygen, we could all wear masks or something," but it was too late. Over two million death threats were received at the stadium where Cormack was due to play, together with 400,000 letter-bombs, and one very badly wrapped poisonous snake which had killed three postal workers en route.

Cormack was undeterred by the threats, largely because the gross ticket receipts for the show came to over one and a half million pounds. He was advised to cancel by his manager, his band, the President of Brazil, the Security Council of the United Nations, Sting, Mother Teresa and Douglas Hurd but, ignoring all their advice, he took the stage at 8pm as planned. This was a brilliant move. Taking the stage at the exact time shown on the ticket was a masterstroke; assuming that there was no prospect of an 8pm rock concert starting till at least 8.40, the audience were all still in the bar. Cormack whipped through his entire repertoire in ten minutes and buggered off back to Britain as fast as the plane could fly.

chapter 9

MONEY FOR NOTHING
Many rock stars have found new creative impetus from the works of leading psychologists. Both John Lennon and Tears For Fears found artistic inspiration from Arthur Janov, proponent of "Primal Therapy", while the title of the Police's 1983 album *Synchronicity* is taken from the works of Carl Jung. It was to Jung that Cormack turned at this time.

"I am currently very interested in the Jungian concept of the collective unconscious and its archetypes," he told *Smash Hits*. "I have attempted to use this in my new single, 'Let's Boogie'."

But "Let's Boogie" flopped, and Cormack now descended into what he has called his "dark period", the lost years during which, fuelled by depression and an inability to write, he retreated to Marksham Place and became a recluse. Friends noticed a drop in weight, and worried that Cormack was using "speedballs" – an injected solution of cocaine and heroin. In fact, he was addicted to Rosemary Conley's Hip'n'Thigh diet. For many long, painful months he ate only carefully selected foods, and could be glimpsed wandering around in legwarmers, lost and miserable. Like most addicts, he became self-obsessed, incapable of talking about anything but his own addiction, uninterested in the world around him. He lost touch. Soon he realised, much to his horror, that he had also become one of the "establishment" that he had once fought against. At one point, watching *The Chart Show* one Saturday lunchtime, he caught himself saying, "but there's just no tunes anymore," and realised that he had become an old fart. Interviewed in 1990, he professed to liking the Happy Mondays because "they write proper songs", and that Jason Donovan "had a nice smile and looked clean and smart".

Under these circumstances, there was little Tim could do other than capitalize on his new-found mainstream acceptance. In 1992, he premiered his *M25 Oratorio*, a full-length choral and orchestral work dedicated to "the finest orbital motorway in the world". Although some sections – notably the "Dominum Nostrum Heathrow-Reigate" and the "Kyrie Eleison Dartford" – were deemed to be successful, the *Daily Telegraph* summed up most of the reviews when it described it as: "another attempt by a pop musician to gain cultural significance through feeble pastiche of the classical genre." Cormack was delighted by this review, until someone explained what it meant.

What does the future hold? Recently, Cormack has made appearances on *Noel's House Party* and accepted a commission to write the soundtrack of *Basil the Great Mouse Detective 2*. He has also described Nirvana as "looking in need of a good wash" and expressed his "disgust" at the "four-letter words" used by Suede. His new album, *Isn't It A Shame About Charles and Diana?*, is due out in the New Year.

SEX

"Fascinating, seminal, medically justified, and in no way just back-door soft-porn like most of these books."

THE
Victorian
LOVERS' GUIDE

A full, frank and explicit guide to better lovemaking (1893 edition) by Cornelius Uptite-Forskeyn

FULLY ILLUSTRATED

INTRODUCTION

It is an unfortunate fact of life that, in order to propagate children, it is necessary for men and women to conjoin and know each other in a carnal sense. As St Paul tells us in the Bible, it would be better if we could all be celibate, but sadly, this is not the case.

Sexual relations are, of course, wicked and sinful, and every effort should be made to minimize them. However, since it is necessary, in order to produce an heir, to engage in this vile and odious practice, I feel that this book may be justified. Our society, quite rightly, keeps information on this disreputable and disgusting topic to an absolute minimum, but when a gentleman and gentlewoman become conjoined in marriage, it is sadly necessary that they are told the physical details of what is involved. I have seen many fine, upstanding couples lose their estates to cousins, merely because they genuinely expected a stork to arrive bearing their offspring. I know of one gentleman who, on being told what he would have to do to produce a son, enlisted in the Army sooner than lower himself to such depravity.

The Author: a Sexual Athlete

It is my fervent hope and belief that in another hundred years' time, we shall possess techniques for the elimination of the horrible function of sexual intercourse altogether. I am comforted by the thought that, for our descendants in 1993, life will be a pleasanter, cleaner and more morally uplifiting experience. In the meantime, though, the filth must continue. I trust that this volume may perhaps alleviate the distress that I know it causes to many British men and women whose lives would otherwise be perfectly wholesome and decent.

56   *CORNELIUS UPTITE-FORSKEYN*

Chapter One

THE NECESSITY FOR DEPRAVITY AND FILTH

Avoiding Masturbation: Technique 1

Avoiding Masturbation: Technique 2

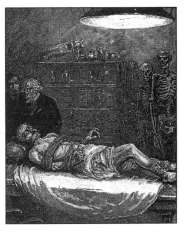

Avoiding Masturbation: Technique 3

In a repressive age, subtle techniques are needed to indicate sexual desire

In order to indulge in filth it is necessary for the gentleman to select a lady to indulge with, or vice versa. London provides gentlemen with ample opportunity to eye up the talent.

Having selected a young woman of good breeding and impeccable morals, it is then necessary to woo, court and walk out with her.

A stylish dresser will always prove irresistible to the opposite sex

Next, one must gain the permission of her father for her hand in marriage. Here, the important thing is to demonstrate your personal wealth and prospects. No gentleman will allow his daughter to marry a man destined for poverty.

When confronted by a nymphomaniac, retain dignity at all times

Having accomplished all this, you may proceed to the nasty business of the filth.

Before entering into marriage, the young gentleman should acquaint himself with the task that lies ahead.

Many gentlemen are surprised and shocked to find that a lady is materially different to a gentleman in various ways.

These ways will become apparent to you when you are both disrobed in the privacy of your marital chamber. It is beyond my capabilities to bring myself to utter them here.

Do not feel embarrassed when purchasing condoms

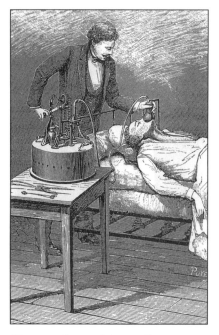

Many gentlemen faint on first seeing their wife naked. However, they can be quickly revived with oxygen, and things can proceed

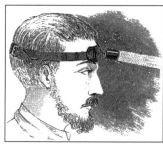

Many men worry about finding their wife in the dark

Do not let first-night nerves ruin your honeymoon

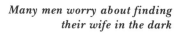

Chapter Two

THE ACTUAL FILTH ITSELF

The only way for gentlemen and gentlewomen to approach the subject is by frank and explicit discussion of what is involved.

There are a number of different "positions" in which intercourse may take place:

1. STANDING POSITION

The gentleman stands a distance apart from the lady. They may smile at each other, and converse politely on suitable subjects.

2. SITTING POSITION

Both partners shall sit in chairs at a slight angle to each other. Many people find this both comfortable and decorous.

3. THE "WHEELBARROW"

The garden is a most pleasant environment in which ladies and gentlemen may mingle in pleasant surroundings. It is best to stay on the path, to avoid muddying one's shoes.

Attract women with amusing tricks

Some women like their husbands to dress up for sex

Chapter Three

ADVANCED TECHNIQUES FOR AROUSAL

It is the duty of every stout-hearted, God-fearing British man and woman to ensure that both themselves and their partner derive as little pleasure from filth as possible. It is quite possible that, perhaps without even knowing it, you are giving pleasure to your partner. If this is so, there are various techniques which, with a little practice, will ensure that your heirs can be fertilized with as little chance of enjoyment as possible:

1. VOMITING ON YOUR PARTNER

If your partner emits any noises, or shows any signs that they are enjoying themselves whilst in the middle of filth, you may find that being sick on them very effectively prevents this from continuing.

To prevent you from hearing your wife's pleasure, strap two After-Eight mints to your ears

2. SINGING THE NATIONAL ANTHEM

Many couples find that, in order immensely to decrease their enjoyment, mutual loud singing of the National Anthem is very good.

3. LACK OF WASHING

An excellent technique, known the world over, for keeping your partner's pleasure to a minimum is to not wash for several days, or preferably several weeks beforehand. Gentlemen may find that if you

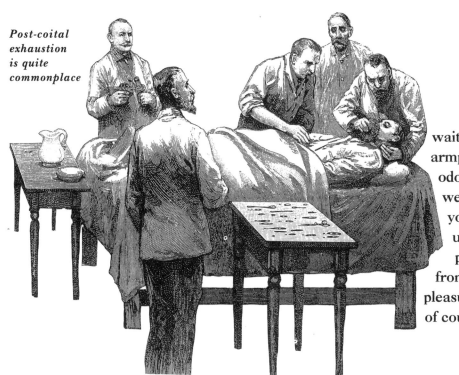

Post-coital exhaustion is quite commonplace

wait long enough, your armpits will be so odorous that you may well anaesthetize your wife into unconsciousness, preventing her from taking any pleasure at all. This is, of course, excellent.

Some gentlemen may develop more sophisticated sexual tastes

BESTSELLING FICTION

"Another epic masterpiece from one of Britain's best-loved writers of this sort of stuff."

The Rune Sword of Trollsbane

Book 1 of the Elvenchant Trilogy, the second Trilogy in the first Part of the Gryphonthrone Saga, the second Saga in the first Part of the final Volume of the Chronicles of Oldenland, the second Chronicle in the great History of the Wars of the Under-Earth*

* All 314 titles available in paperback. If you cannot find the one you want, don't worry, they're all the same.

From the Same Author:

The Gryphonthrone Saga – Part One

THE GNOMESONG TRILOGY
The Wizard's Staff Breaks
Questors of the Wizard's Staff
The Wizard's Staff is Mended

THE ELVENCHANT TRILOGY
The Runesword of Trollsbane
The Trollsword of Runebane
The Banesword of Trollrune

THE PIXIEBALLAD TRILOGY
To the Fortress of Mordrac
Flight from the Fortress of Mordrac
Back to the Fortress of Mordrac

The Gryphonthrone Saga – Part Two

THE DWARFROUNDEL TRILOGY
The Runeshield Goes West
The Runeshield Goes East
The Runeshield Gets Lost

THE FAERIERAP TRILOGY
Sorceror of the Gryphonthrone
Rune-Cauldron of the Sorceror
Sorceror on the Job

THE TROLLANTHEM TRILOGY
Dragontroll Quest
The Crystal Dragontroll
Dragontrolls Go Ape!!

AUTHOR'S NOTE

Concerning the History, Peoples and Languages of Oldenland

Oldenland is the area of the Under-Earth that lies between the Frozen Wilderness and the Place of Sands. It is bordered to the East by the Great Water, and to the West by the impenetrable tundra of Hinter. Oldenland itself is divided into the five great Kingdoms – Eldendor, Magdenor, Vangoria, Putridia and Elphanenroth.

The Great Wars of the Under-Earth began in the third millennium of Ton-Dor, when the forces of Putridia invaded Eldendor and built the mighty Dark Fortress of Gok, which stood for two thousand elf-years before it was destroyed by Ranwak the Brave at the Battle of Horlix Pass. During the occupation of Eldendor, King Borax the Bald had to flee into the Haunted Mountains, while his son, Anusol, joined the dwarf-armies of Magdenor. However, during the Second Era of the Beasts, the terrible Mordrac, ruler of the Dark Lands of Barf, enslaved the mighty wizard Tixylix, forcing him to bend his magical powers to the uses of evil.

With Tixylix now under his command, Mordrac controlled all the dreaded Slimeworms of the Dank Catacombs of Harpic, together with Flob, the giant ten-legged tarantula which patrolled the Mentadent Pass into the Valleys of Snarge. In this way, Anusol was captured and the kingdoms of Magdenor and Elvendor were set at war with each other. The beautiful Princess Liana, half-sister of Moonwringer the White Witch, then set off to rescue Anusol.

Using her half-sister's magical powers, she disguised herself as a Swiss Cheese plant in order to enter Mordrac's Fortress of Eternal Doom. For although the Fortress had walls eight yards thick, towers five hundred feet high, and was guarded by the most ferocious trolls and orc-beasts from the Ash Forests of Putridia, it definitely lacked anything in the way of ornamental house-plants. (Mordrac had even fallen for the trick before, during the Third War of the Raven's Beak, when Haliborange, prince of

Vangoria, had given him a gift of an asparagus fern. Since no living thing would voluntarily cross the threshold of the Fortress, the fern had to be packed into a sealed box and told it was going somewhere else. Once inside, the fern – which had been placed under a spell by Ingolf the Warlock – changed itself into a mighty Grobnar-tree, destroying the Powerstone of Orlon, and leaving Mordrac powerless for three-score years.)

Such was the legend told by the wandering minstrels of Elphanenroth, until one fateful day, a small, frightened gnome called Korbut appeared in the Western March of Eldendor, claiming to have seen great Snargebeasts moving through the Forests of Dando. Then came the terrible news that the great staff of Tixylix's distant descendant, Meketrix, had snapped in half while he was cleaning it. The coming of the Snargebeasts together with the breaking of the wizard's staff fulfilled the first part of an ancient prophecy which predicted the mightiest conflict of all – the great final struggle between the dark forces of Putridia, and the assorted gnomes, elves, dwarves and woodland folk, who must be victorious if they were to carry on their peaceful lives, sitting on toadstools and playing merry elvish pranks. Thus began the great Wars of Under-Earth.

The peoples of Under-Earth are many and varied. Elvendor is mainly populated by elves, who are swift, woodland creatures, skilled in magic, and fond of singing, poetry and badminton. They have a strange fondness for fromage frais, particularly apricot flavour, which they call *aphelennoh dellofel* – the "bollocks of the dog".

Magdenor is the kingdom of the dwarves, creatures of the earth, cave-dwellers, skilled with stone, forgers of mighty battle-axes, strong, loyal, fearless, but almost invariably allergic to milk. This is their only weakness in war, and can make them unreliable allies. Although they are ruthless fighters, and their armour is impenetrable by arrow or blade, you only have to pour a pint of semi-skimmed over their heads and they start wheezing and breaking out in a rash.

Vangoria is the land of the faeries: tough, hard-fighting creatures whose gauzy wings and little sparkly tutus belie a warlike nature. Spingle-Spangle, King of Faerieland, is celebrated in minstrel songs as being "hard as nails", while the Honeynectar of Atora is almost 8.7% proof and drunk exclusively in quarts. At the Battle of the Seven Rivers, the faeries would not ride the swift Horses of the Horan Plains offered by King Creole, preferring instead to use their Kawasaki 850's. Pewk, the Prince of Faeriedom, once fought against the Sacred Deathsword of Kron-Dor armed only with a bike-chain.

Elphanenroth is a strange kingdom, a place of dragonmoths, the Heron-People of Gorlak, and the fearsome Fighting Frogs ("Who dares, croaks"). Travellers may encounter the Egg-Men of Tranwar, or the mysterious gnomes who, on the night of a full moon, will appear in sequinned bodysuits and perform Latin ballroom routines in the Lost Valleys of Randol. There are also pixies, who are quite the most unpleasant creatures. Pixies are the most sexually perverted of all the Oldenland-dwellers. Old pixies enjoy flashing, and will jump out at travellers stark naked except for a red pointy hat and a long grey beard, which they will lift up to reveal horrible, gnarled old pixie tackle. (A pixie-penis is bright red with white spots. It evolved in this way as camouflage, so that pixies could lie on their backs in forests and masturbate without anyone noticing.)

Visitors may also encounter the terrible Chartered Sirens of the Rocks, who entice weary travellers with their tempting promises of cheap accountancy, only to send them to their doom at the hands of the dreaded VATman of Gorgolon.

Across the icy peaks of the Meddling Mountains is the terrible kingdom of Putridia, land of the Dark Forces, home of Mordrac the Wicked. Mordrac, with his legions of Venom-Bats, his armies of wild Skunk-Lizards ("Who dares, farts") and battalions of fierce Short-Haired Killer-Trolls, is almost invincible, apart from his fatal weakness for house-plants.

There are many languages and dialects in use in Oldenland. There is the General Tongue, which is used by the races when they want to communicate with each other, but is clumsy, unpoetic, and makes everyone snicker because of the juvenile sexual innuendo.

The Elvish languages are used for songs and poetry, and are very beautiful – words like *alphendendroleppilidon* ("spoon") or *happedrolendonnemon* ("carpet underlay") possessing a quality of joy in words. Visitors to Elvendor would need phrases like *remeldendron alphaphor marendendrosscribor* ("I am a stranger") or *wellenfroth dirralirramirra stammerkru?* ("Can you tell me the way to the nearest post-office, please?").

In contrast, trolls have a vocabulary of only 50 words, 37 of which mean "kill" or "death". The faerie tongue is notoriously difficult to understand, containing 6 different genders, 14 cases, 28 different verb-tenses, and a system of personal and impersonal pronouns which change according to who you're talking to, how well you know them, whether it's morning or afternoon, and whether or not the sentence involves a transitive or intransitive verb. There are 11 different third-person singular versions of the verb "to be"; adjectives have to agree with nouns in number, case and gender; and the rules are slightly different between spoken and written sentences. This is compounded by the fact that if you make a grammatical mistake in front of a faerie, they will beat you up. It is generally best to mime.

CONTENTS

PART FOUR   The Flight to the Fort

PART FIVE   The Last Battle

Where Mordrac's eye doth fall upon
The trees do fade and die
Where Mordrac's breath doth faintly touch
It smells worse than shit-pie.

So forge the Sword!
The Sword of Runes!
In dwarf-forge's red-heat!
Forge the Runesword!
If you don't
You are, basically, dead meat.

Ancient Song of Elvendor's Quarg-Minstrels

(We regret that due to the inclusion of Additional Available
Titles, Map, Author's Note, Contents, and Poem, we do not have space
for the actual story. Sorry.)

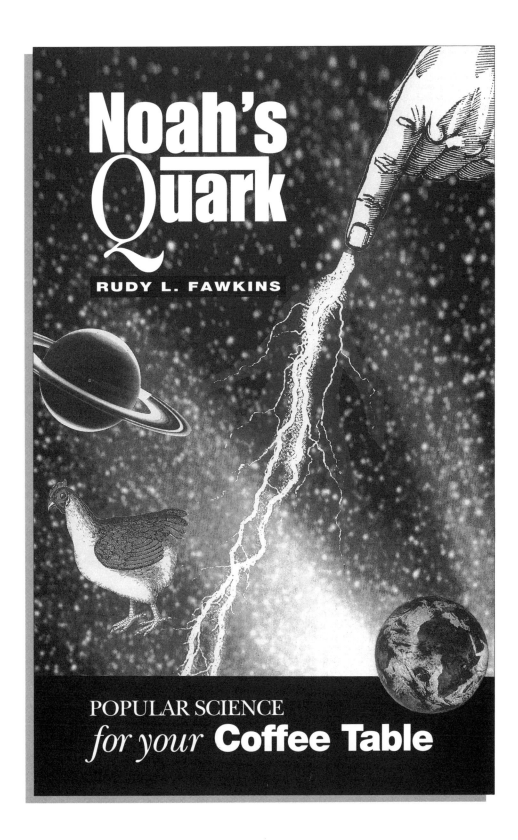

"In a crowded market, this book sticks out like a neutron in a vacuum."

Noah's Quark

RUDY L. FAWKINS

POPULAR SCIENCE
for your **Coffee Table**

INTRODUCTION

At 7.34 pm on 4th November, 1988, Tom Schmidt was idly watching the monitor-screen of a proton-disintegration scanner in the Physical Science Laboratory at the University of North Dakota, when he suddenly noticed an abnormality on the VDU.

He could not know that 6000 miles away, in the People's Laboratory for Particle Physics in Smolensk, USSR, Dr Sergei Prlepkov and Ivan Terovitch were looking on in incredulity as their particle-accelerator showed definite signs of an electron-tracking discharge-malfunction. Careful examination showed that, far from being a malfunction, the accelerator had in fact picked up visible evidence of a previously unknown particle.

And neither of the two groups could possibly realise that, in Woking, England, the Fourth Years at Addlestone Comprehensive were about to heat some copper sulphate over a bunsen burner.

All of which goes to prove one thing: *Science isn't dull*.

No indeed. Science is an adventure, a crazy rock'n'roll roller-coaster journey through the mind. Most people tend to think of scientists as geeky guys in glasses who spend their time crouched over test-tubes, but hey! You're mondo wrongo, pal. These days, your average research scientist is more likely to be a crazy gonzoid mutha who's out there on the edge, chasing those particles, finding those quasars, getting hold of some mindbending quantum concept and *kicking its ass*.

Leading scientists these days are *characters*, and you'd better believe it. These eggheads are big-time, man. These guys and gals are *stars*. TV, books, you name it, your major research scientist these days is doin' it. And after I read Professor Screamin' Jay Dawkins' *Chromosome Like it Hot*, and Bernard P. Rawkins' *Primeval Soup Bowl*, and Simon K. Pawkins' *Big Gang-Bang: Multiple-Universe Creation Theory*, and Garfield B. Kawkins' *Hey! You! Get Offa My Helium Cloud*, I thought, man! These guys are on a mission from God. The public *dig* this stuff. They may not understand it. They may not even *read* it. They may just stick it on their coffee-tables and *pretend* they've read it. But who cares, man? Science is *hep*, it's kicking, and I wanted to write a book that not only explained to the average reader about the most up-to-date scientific theory, but also makes it *groove*.

I wanna make your brain ache, can you dig that? I wanna make these concepts clear and accessible to everyone, even people whose most intellectual reading to date is the lyric-sheet of *Take That and Party*. Because, brothers and sisters, these advances in science are for *you*. The world you live in, the cars you drive, the medicines you take, all of them come from Science. And if I can help you wrap your brain around the frontiers of human knowledge, then I will have achieved what I set out to do. So yo! Let's kick it.

Rudy. L. Fawkins
The Synchotron Particle-Collider, somewhere in Minnesota

CHAPTER ONE

In order for the layman to appreciate the full beauty and majesty of the discoveries made over the last few years, it is necessary to re-cap on a few things about science:

1. The universe is made of very small things.
2. It doesn't look like it is, because these small things club together to make very big things.

The small things are called "atoms" and the big things are called "whales". Or "mountains". Or planets, or dressing-tables, or bananas. Whatever. OK?

Now, here's the catch. The small things, the atoms, aren't actually that small, because they in turn are made up of even smaller things. These things are so small you can't see them, you can only see where they go. Similarly, some of the big things are really big: you know, like, really very big indeed. Like the biggest thing of all is, like, *the universe*, man. That's a big sucker. Blow your mind, man.

But let's get back to the small things. Basically, there are three of these – neutrons, electrons and protons. Now, you're saying to yourself, "proton, schmoton. I don't wanna hear about that. I did that at school, man. Give me the good stuff." OK, so, quarks. Heard of these little muthas, man? Betcha you have. Sure you have. So, you say, what's the deal? Ok, so the deal is, six types, ok? – *up*, *down*, *top*, *bottom*, *strange*, and *charm*. They interact because of a "colour" on each in a way analogous to the interaction between charged particles. Baryons

Dr. Heinrich Drubler-Wubler discovers a dark-ish liquid

are made of three quarks; mesons of quark-antiquark pairs. Still with me? Of course you aren't. Wait till I tell you about quantum chromodynamics, a widely accepted theory of strong nuclear force in which quarks are bound together by gluons. You're lost now. You can't catch up on several centuries of experimental thinking just by buying one paperback. But stick with it, man.

"OK," you say, "what about relativity? That's what I want to know." Well, first let me tell you that Professor Nathan K. Bawkins used to give his lectures on General Relativity dressed as General Custer. That's how crazy *he* was, man. What a character! Ok, so here's the deal. First of all, light. Think of a torch. Switch it on, light comes out. You see that light 'cos it's travelling at a constant speed. Now imagine the torch is strapped to the front of a Maserati, man, and a-headin' right for ya. Y'all think that light's going faster? It's the big N-O, no, man. See, the speed of light is constant for any observer. Understand that? Good, because that's the only thing about relativity you will understand. That's the only thing about relativity that anyone understands, apart from people like me, who can

Bodies of matter held together by their own gravity with a nuclear fusion core. Does your head in, really

understand all those friggin' spaghetti-equations that my publisher told me to steer well clear of.

Light travels in waves. Remember that from school? Imagine, then, that you're *surfin' on light*. It's the ultimate high, man. You're surfin' on a wave of light. You're goin' at 186,000 miles a second and after a hour you look round and no-one back on the beach has moved a muscle, man. 'Cos you're riding the very wave of light you're seeing them with! Time stands still at the speed of light! Can you dig that? Einstein could, man. He was one crazy mutha. He thought all this shit up by *himself*, man, that's how much of a crazy mutha *he* was.

But here's the catch. Light's not just a wave, it's a particle at the same time. Hey, whoa, slow down! What do you mean? What I mean is, that in quantum field theory all matter and force particles are expressed as sums over simple waves. Charged sub-atomic particles interact via photons, the quantum of electromagnetic radiation.

At this point, you're probably saying to yourself – what is this shit? I know the scene, man. You bought this book 'cos you wanna know the answers to basic questions, like what is the universe made of, how did it begin, where is it going? And I'm telling you. But, in all probability, you can't follow it. And that pisses you off. Just hang in there. There's more.

I want to lay something on you. You're gonna love this. Do you know anything about quantized orbital motion of electrons in a magnetic field? See, the conductivity has values that are integer multiples of e^2/h, where e is the electrical charge and h is Planck's constant. Well, hot diggety dog! I know what you're thinking. You're thinking, this is like some heavy deal, man. This is the basic problem with a book like this. You've got to come away with the impression that not knowing that the proposed quantum of gravitation is gravitational interaction via the exchange of gravitons doesn't make you dumb.

Tell you what. Let's go for a visual metaphor. This is the best way we scientists can get a concept across. Think of a bowl of Rice Krispies. Imagine each Rice Krispie is an electron. Then you accelerate those Rice Krispies to near-lightspeeds in a state-of-the-art cyclotron-collider. What happens? You get broken Rice Krispies, man. I don't know if that's any help to you.

CHAPTER TWO

Up to this point, you've probably been thinking, "I don't know shit." Well, now I'm gonna take you quickly through the history of science, and how we came to know all this stuff. And that's gonna make you feel even worse, because you're gonna think, "they understood things four hundred years ago I don't even understand now! I think I'll just give up!" Well, look at it this way – at least you've bought a pop-science book, man. So at least you're interested in finding out how dumb you are.

Most people don't get that far. They did a survey recently in Britain and they found a quarter of the population didn't know that the earth went round the sun. And these people wonder why they can't get jobs, man. Think they're so damned smug because they can pre-program a video-recorder or get rid of a headache, but let me tell you – most people, man, they know dick-all. They drive their cars and watch their televisions but without scientists to make those things work, these people'd still be wrestling mammoths, man. Clubbing each other with flint-axes. Then they have the nerve to start tellin' me and my good-buddies that we're arrogant and presumptuous and all that shit. I tell you what people hate, man – they hate feeling stupid. And even reading a book like this makes the average person feel stupid, let alone glancing through a copy of *Mass-Spectroscopy Weekly* or some other science journal, man.

DINOSAURS: Rock 'n'roll animals. Live fast, die young, leave a good-looking fossil

They can't understand it, so they don't want no-one else to understand it either. They start going on about how we play God. Because that's nice and easy to understand, religion. Any dumb-ass can grasp that one. Everything got made by this nice God dude, he looks after us, we don't die.

Simple. Supposed to be simple. Designed to be simple. Whereas, man, what these people don't realise is that if God is anything, he ain't simple. God is one complex mutha, man. See, these religious freaks who think the world was made in six days and all the animals and stuff – they don't agree with evolution, but, see, what they're missing out on, man, through their fear of feeling stupid, is that science is more awesome than anything in religion. Turning water into wine? That's Paul Daniels, man. You want a miracle, then get Jesus to turn amino acids and nucleic acids into DNA. If God exists, man – and I ain't saying he don't – then he is subtle and complex. He don't just plonk everything down in a week and say "that's it". This is the great thing about science, man. See, you read the Bible, and you keep being told, "you're human, and humans don't know shit". But you read science, and you don't need to be told. You *know* you don't know shit.

CHAPTER THREE

Evolution, man. That's a tricky one. Kinda controversial, too. A lot of people find it hard to grasp, largely because they don't really want to grasp it. Because it's kinda frightening. See, what humans have always kinda believed is two basic things:

1) Humans are the highest species because we have a "soul".
2) We are here for a reason.

Quite what reason, they never say. Apparently God made the earth as a kind of bio-moral experiment lab, so he could see how we get on, and we live, rather pointlessly, for sixty or seventy years or whatever, and on the basis of that, we get the rest of eternity either with him or somewhere else. Or rather, our "soul" does. Now, what evolution says is that the process of life is a blind series of chemical reactions and that when we die we moulder away.

See, there's a kinda weird irony here, man. Religion says that the body dies but the soul lives on. Science says that the soul dies but the body lives on. See, the "soul" – that's bullshit, man. That's conscious-

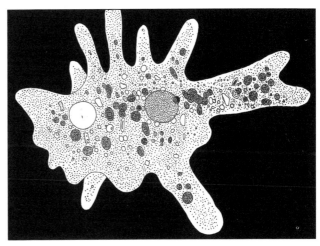

EVOLUTION: 500 million years ago we all looked like this. Drop enough acid and we still do

ness. That's what dies. The body gets immortality, because you can't create or destroy matter. So all your atoms live on, man. Only, obviously, that's not a lot of use to you. But Nature has only lent you your atoms for the duration. They've got other shit to do, man. No self-respecting carbon atom wants to hang around being your nose or your ear or something, when it could be off becoming a pencil or a tree or some shit like that. So you get kinda metaphorical immortality. But that's not good enough for us humans. We're so damned arrogant, we think we deserve not to die just for having been born human. I tell you what religion is. It's species-Nazism, man. We are the master-race. We already took over the whole damn planet as *lebensraum*. We already put plenty other species in the ovens, man. Because we are the Chosen Ones. That's what religion says. It says we have dominion over the birds of the air and the beasts of the field. In other words, we can

Two bio-chemists try to work out what on earth they're doing

kill 'em and eat 'em, poison their homes, trap 'em, sacrifice 'em, because we are the master-race. We're species-Nazis. We are created in God's own image. In other words, God looks human. All the other stuff is on the planet for us to eat or put in cages.

Now, evolution says different. Evolution says we're just another animal. But we are a very successful one. We are, in fact, the master-race. But not because no-one made us that way. We *developed* that way. We just happened to be on the end of a branch of land-dwelling, tree-climbing, fast-moving, dextrous mammals who were good at not getting themselves eaten and shit like that. And now we're enjoying a short period of success as rulers of this planet, before we poison ourselves and blow ourselves up and generally blow the whole scam by overpopulating and polluting and all that stuff, man.

So okay. You say, "Right. I don't buy this Creation riff, man. It don't satisfy me, intellectually or rationally, and, somehow, it's just too trite. I want something awesome, man. Freak me out." OK, man, dig this. Evolution works through mutation. Heritable changes are very infrequent, because the structure of deoxyribonucleic acid is very stable. Deoxy-what? DNA, man. It's a nucleic acid, which occurs in combination with protein in the chromosomes, consists of four primary nitrogenous bases (adenine, guanine, thymine, and cytosine), 2-deoxy-D-ribose, and phosphoric acid. And according to the Bible God thought that lot up in a *day*, man. So, dig, this groovy stuff consists of two chains of alternate sugar and phosphate groups twisted round each other into a double helix. Every human cell contains 6×10^9 base pairs of DNA, that's about six-and-a-half feet of it, but coiled on itself again and again so it fits inside the nucleus of the cell, and that is *small*, man. Then there's this other shit called RNA which carries out all the instructions of the DNA and it's only when any of this goes wrong that you get a mutant, man – and evolution is driven by mutants. You got some primeval friggin' fish, man, and it lives off eating other, little tiny fish, and then suddenly one day wham! The DNA screws up. It replicates slightly differently and accidentally sends out the instruction "Grow Bigger Teeth". And some friggin' mother-fish is looking at her offspring and thinking Shit! These ugly-mugs are my *kids*? Jesus, I'm so

EVOLUTION: You can dig where Darwin's coming from

embarrassed! And all the other fish laugh at these goofy-looking fish with big teeth, and what happens? The fish with the big teeth get kinda pissed off and turn round and *eat* all the others. 'Cos they suddenly find that having big teeth means they can eat whatever they friggin' choose, man. These muthas don't have to eat no friggin' *plankton* and shit. These muthas can eat Big Mac and fries if they want, 'cos they've got big friggin' teeth. Pretty soon all the other fish are saying "Don't mess with the toothy fish. They are mean bastard fish, man. Bite your friggin' head off." So the toothy fish get all big and strong and have lots of toothy kids, and pretty soon all the

78

species got big teeth, because all the ones that ain't got 'em are friggin' dead, man. They is fish-food. This is called natural selection. This is what produced us, man. Humans.

See, Charles Darwin, all these Jesus-freaks really hated him, man, 'cos he was the first one who stood up and said, "We are not special. We are basically gorillas who've learnt to shave." And everybody said, "You is crazy, man. You is some friggin' crazy man. This is the most totally bogus horseshit we ever heard. You're saying we're monkeys?" And Darwin said, "Yes, man." And the Pope goes ape, and there's the Scopes trial and PG Tips get this great idea for a commercial and shit like that.

So, not only are we apes, but we are like mutant-apes, man. This is some weird shit, but stick with it. See, it's natural selection again. 'Cos our ancestors lived in like trees, and they had enemies, man. You think it's bad now with the police pulling you over for driving with no rear-light and the Inland Revenue hassling you, but that's got to be better than the crap our ancestors had to put up with. People moan they can't walk the city streets at night but your average law-abiding gorilla couldn't walk the friggin' *forest* at night. 'Cos they got *mugged*. You think it's bad being mugged by some crack-head with a knife? You try being mugged by a friggin' *sabre-toothed tiger*. This mutha don't even want your watch and wallet, man. He just wants to tear your fuckin' head off and *eat* you and shit like that. And it's not due to social conditions or the creation of a disenfranchised underclass, either. It's due to the fact that he's a sabre-toothed tiger and those muthas have got a bit of DNA that says "tear people's heads off for fun".

OK, so, one day some chimp's DNA mutates and his kids get born with great long arms. And the parents think, oh no. So this mutant monkey's wandering around with his front arms so long that he has to stand almost upright, and he feels really dumb. But one day up comes some sabre-toothed tiger, and all the other monkeys are on all fours so they can't see behind them. But the monkey with the long stupid-looking arms is almost upright and he can turn his head round and he sees the tiger and gets himself up the nearest tree faster than you can say "slavering predator", man. But the others are just foraging around and the sabre-toothed tiger rips their heads off, man. This is how it works. It's like the weirdest shit you ever saw, man. Like freaks like the chameleon, man. It can make itself look like its background. That's 'cos all the chameleons that didn't got eaten.

Ok. So. Someone says to you, "I don't believe in evolution. Prove it to me." Here's the proof, man. It's what we scientists call the Penguin Proof.

Now, the penguin – *Birdus ridiculus* – is renowned in biology for being the world's stupidest-looking bird. Because it is one of a select group of species known as the flightless birds. Another flightless bird was the dodo, and we all know what happened to that. It got clubbed to death by explorers for fun. People today say, "How can they have shown such senseless cruelty?" but, as a scientist, I fully sympathise. If I saw a dodo, I'd club it to death, just to put it out of its misery. Because a flightless bird is a pointless bird. The whole point about birds is that they evolved *wings*. Because then they didn't have to walk. Then, when a friggin' Ice Age started, all the other animals froze to death, but the birds could just fly off somewhere warmer. How many times

PENGUIN: Pointless

have you ever wished you could fly? Everyone would like to fly. Flying is one of the great archetypal race-dreams of human-beings, and thus of mammals everywhere. Yet the miserable penguin was able to fly but *couldn't be friggin' bothered*. So, in time, its wings wasted away. What can you *say* about a species like that?

79

Why did the penguin not want to fly? I'll tell you why, man. Because it lives in the friggin' Antarctic. And there's *nowhere* to go. Everywhere looks the *same*. It's all snow, man, and ice. You take off, you look down – you can't tell where the fuck you are. A penguin would think, "Right. I've got these wings. I'll go somewhere." So he takes off, he flies for a bit, he gets completely lost. Everything looks the same. It's just snow. No landmarks. No nothing. Just millions of square miles of white. Penguin freaks out. Penguin lands. Penguin starves to death.

Not surprisingly, after a while, all the other penguins start thinking: "Hang on. Not one *single one* of our brethren who has ever flown anywhere has ever come back. This flying shit is overrated, man. It's okay for eagles and stuff, who've got mountains and streams to fly over. All we've got is friggin' snow."

So, in the absence of navigational aids, the penguin decided to stop trying to fly places, and instead to get about by waddling around in that stupid waddly way. I don't know if it happened exactly like that, but we can never know the exact truth, just like we can never know what convinced the walrus to grow those stupid tusks. I mean – what *is* that? Ok, so there was a DNA mutation and one of them grew tusks. All the others took one look and said, "you are the ugliest muthafucker in the whole friggin' Southern hemisphere, man." So why did they all want them too? What *is* that?

BATS: Just plain weird

Science is full of these mysteries. That's why it's such an excellent subject, man. Full of weirdness and utter strangeness, and inexplicably mysterious stuff and shit.

Take bats, man. Bats are the freakiest species on the planet. Whenever anyone asks me why I don't believe God created the world, I cite, as Exhibit A, the bat. Because my thinking is this, man. If God created the bat, then God is weird. And I don't like the idea of a weird God. God should be reliable and stable, and wear a cardigan and stuff.

Bats, man. Wacksville, Arizona. OK, so some creatures evolved to be nocturnal, 'cos then none of the other animals can see them and they can hunt without being hunted and all that stuff. Most creatures that evolved nocturnal developed like powerful eyes so they can see in the dark. Sort of like infra-red vision. But that wasn't good enough for the bat. No. The bat – get this – sees by friggin' *sonar*.

I *cannot* believe God did this. I mean, he's only got one day to create all the animals. He's got enough work on his hands, he's not gonna stop halfway through and say, "Hang on. Tell you what we haven't got yet, and that's a hang-gliding gerbil that thinks it's a submarine."

Because that's what a friggin' bat is, man. It's a rodent with attitude. A rodent who thinks, scurrying about down sewers is not for me. I want to *fly*, man. And I don't want none of this eyes business. I want to see through my *ears*.

You know what a bat does? It sends out sound-waves out of its friggin' head, and those sound waves bounce off things, and then they go back to the bat and it picks 'em up and from that it can judge distances, it can build up a sound-picture in its head and it can fly about at night at high speed with its eyes shut *without hitting anything*. I mean, this is some seriously weird shit, isn't it? This is some freak-mutha of a mammal. How on earth did that evolve?

This is the sort of question that Science sets out to answer. But what the answer is exactly, we don't know. And even if we did, it would be very hard to explain to the layman. That's the problem. But hey. Let's talk about quasars, man...!

"The conclusions of this book will shock, astonish and worry you. It is perhaps the most significant title to emerge since a few weeks ago."

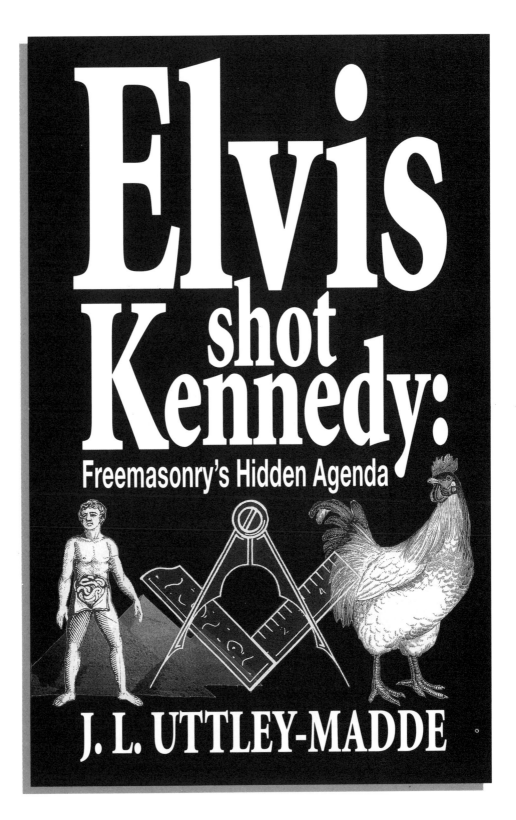

Elvis shot Kennedy:
Freemasonry's Hidden Agenda

J. L. UTTLEY-MADDE

INTRODUCTION

In 1981 I was working as a junior researcher on the BBC2 documentary series *Horizontal* when my producer – a quiet, mild-mannered man called Milton King – was suddenly found in his office impaled on a large spear. A series of strange cuts on his chest formed the shape of an inverted equilateral triangle, and the word "Rache" was painted in blood on his wall-planner.

This set me thinking.

King had recently begun working on a programme investigating time-share sales practices in the South of France. Could there possibly be a link? It was hard to believe that any time-share salesman would carry out a ritual slaying with a four-foot spear.

The matter was referred upwards within the BBC. Tony Plinge, the then Assistant Head of Documentary Features, dismissed the cold-blooded killing as "not an appropriate subject" for a documentary programme, suggesting that we took it instead to *That's Life*. This we did, and on November 14th of that year a brief item was broadcast, in which passers-by were stopped and asked if any of them knew anybody who had been speared by a time-share salesman. The press carried a few small stories, but were more interested in the item which followed (a roller-skating parrot which knew all the words to "Don't You Want Me?" by the Human League). And there, it seemed, the matter would rest.

And yet there were still one or two unanswered questions. Then, one morning, a letter arrived in the office. It had been sent anonymously from Switzerland. The contents were in Latin, and read:

REX MORTIS EST
("King is dead")

It seemed obvious enough. Milton King was indeed dead. But then I idly realised that, in Latin, nouns do not, as in English, have to take an article. Hence "King is dead" might equally be taken to mean "The King is dead". But which king?

I thought about this. Perhaps this was a reference to Henry the Eighth? He was certainly dead. So was William the Conqueror – in fact, he had been dead considerably longer. Indeed, I could not think of a single King of England who was not currently dead: George III, Richard II, Charles I – all six feet under. Foreign kings were the same. All dead, apart from the ones who were alive. It didn't seem to make any sense.

It was then that I remembered – from a chance remark on the radio – that "The King" might not refer to a literal monarch at all. It was around 10.15 one morning at Television Centre, and Simon Bates was doing "Our Tune" on the radio. At the end of the story – which concerned a girl whose boyfriend had drowned in a jacuzzi on their wedding night – I clearly remember Simes saying, "And to this day Carol's heart still misses a beat when she hears this tune. It's the King, with "Heartbreak Hotel".

Of course! "The King" was the nickname of Elvis Presley. And Elvis Presley was dead!

All this seemed to have far-reaching implications. What those implications were I was not quite sure, but I was on the threshold of an incredible jounrney of discovery. It started the next day, when I related all this to my Head of Department. He sacked me on the spot, with the advice that I should take a long holiday.

Which is precisely what I did, for my mind was in a whirl. Could there be any connection between the death of my producer and the deaths of Elvis Presley, President Kennedy and Marilyn Monroe? And could there be any connection between a dodgy time-share company, and the medieval order of warrior-monks, the Knights Templar? And could any of this lead to a shattering secret that would force us to re-think everything we know about Christianity? For I knew that if I could establish such a connection, I could probably blag a large advance out of a publisher, and write a book about it.

This is that book.

CHAPTER ONE
The Conspiracy Unfolds

Historically, the Establishment has always reacted fiercely in defence of the status quo. Any brave soul who is bold enough to re-assemble the facts to fit a new, challenging hypothesis regarding any of the conventional "truths" about our society is liable to be ridiculed, vilified, and, at the very least, slagged off in the Sunday papers.

So it was with some trepidation that I embarked on my extensive researches which were to lead me down paths which I had not in the least expected, finding connections where I had not even thought to look for them.

I began, naturally enough, with a totally open mind. I knew only one thing – that the more outlandish and controversial my book was, the more money I would get. But I did not in any way let this influence the course which my research took.

I wanted, first and foremost, to make sure that my research was academically sound, and could stand up to the most rigorous examination that the forces of Establishment thinking could throw at me. For this reason I went out and bought a copy of *Weird Phenomena that No-one Understands* from my local railway station. This respected volume, published by the internationally renowned Whacko Press, contained many thought-provoking hypotheses: that the world is flat; that the world is hollow; that Bigfoot exists and is telepathic; that UFOs are abducting people who live on remote farms and using them for breeding experiments; and so forth.

One topic especially interested me – the chapter on King Arthur. For so many are the legends surrounding this King that he must have had some basis in fact. Yet no trace of his fabulous Camelot has ever been found. Why? Could it have been demolished?

Then consider the Seven Wonders of the World. Every schoolchild knows that the Colossus of Rhodes, the Pharos (lighthouse) at Alexandria, the Mausoleum of Helicarnassus, the Temple of Artemis at Ephesus, the Statue of Zeus at Olympia, the Hanging Gardens of Babylon and the Pyramids of Egypt are considered by historians and scholars to be the most miraculous structures in the ancient world. What all these structures have in common is that they are all made of stone. It is evident that even when these astonishing achievements were first made, stonemasons must have been immensely powerful people.

All these great structures were built by masons. Masons built the palaces, the temples, the city walls that defended rulers from attack. Masons held huge power, for without skilled stone-workers, a society was primitive. It relied on wood, which rotted and caught fire. Even in Britain, the great structures, from Stonehenge to Hadrian's Wall to the Tower of London to the great cathedrals, were all built by masons. Small wonder, then, that the Society of Freemasons became the most powerful organization in the world. Everybody, from popes to princes, needed stone-workers. The extraordinary mathematical dimensions of the Pyramids, the incredible civil engineering feats of the Hanging Gardens, the great religious shrines – all built by masons.

It is well known that the origins of Freemasonry lie within the mysterious organization of the Knights Templar. This Order – founded by Chretien de Troyes, ostensibly to protect 12th-century pilgrims on their way to Jerusalem – was at one time the richest and most powerful organization in Europe, lending money to kings and owning vast tracts of land. The Order was dissolved after the Knights were accused of doing all manner of naughty things, including the worshipping of a bearded head, the sacrificing of animals, and the building of huge secret undergound labyrinths without proper planning permission. The Knights also seem somehow to have been involved with many other mysterious organizations, strange hermetic sects, Rosicrucians and alchemical occultists. Quite how all this fitted in with my story I did not yet know, but I knew that I had to involve the Knights Templar somehow, since all the other books do.

It seemed already that I had the beginnings of a hypothesis: all the greatest human artefacts – the palaces of the rulers, and the temples of the great religions – relied on the skill of stonemasons to make sure they didn't fall down, or otherwise cause hazards to their occupants. This explained the immense power of the Masons throughout history and the huge power they held over both kings and popes alike.

Imagine! If the Pope argued with the Masons all they needed to say was, "OK, Your Holiness, all your cathedrals will fall down." Similarly, if a king tried to pass laws against them, they could simply remove one key foundation stone, and his palace roof would fall on his head and kill him. This seemed, to me, to be totally logical and it already explained an enormous number of things. For example, scholars have puzzled for centuries over the incredible mathematical complexities of the Pyramids. Even more puzzling, it has been calculated that the Pyramids must have taken at least 150 years to build. Why so long? If they were simply designed to be tombs for Pharaohs, then why would any Pharaoh commission a mausoleum which would not be finished until long after his death?

It was at this point that I found, in the Bibliotheque Nationale in Paris, a small, obscure book, ignored by academics, called *Aliens from Mars Built the Pyramids!!* by Ronnie Cranke. From the first page, it was clear why this book has never been widely available to the public. Its conclusions are too radical and too challenging to the cosy view of the Establishment. Although

I could not agree with Cranke's central theory, there was, however, one very interesting piece of information in the book concerning the "Original Estimate Tablet of Giza".

This stone slab, discovered in the sands near the Great Pyramid in 1925, was covered in hieroglyphics which were to remain undeciphered until the early 1970s, when a team at the University of Minnesota Egyptology Department made the incredible discovery that the tablet did, in fact, show the original builders' estimate for the Great Pyramid, and demonstrated quite clearly that it was originally supposed to be finished in *six months*.

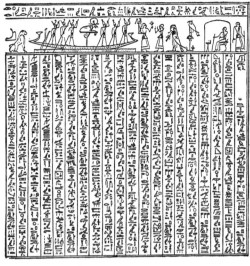

This set me thinking. Why, when the Pyramid was supposed to be built in half a year, did it end up taking three hundred times as long? Could it have been due to plagues, or wars? Did the Nile flood? Was there some cataclysmic upheaval? The answer was much simpler. In fact, it was so simple it was staring me in the face. It was, quite simply, that *builders have not changed in three thousand years.*

Everybody knows that any building project – be it your

The famous "Original Estimate Tablet", found in 1925

kitchen extension at home, or the Channel Tunnel – will never be finished when it is originally supposed to be. The M25, the Humber Bridge, Stansted Airport, all these things were completed years after their original completion date. In the case of the M25, it is still not really finished now. As soon as it was opened, workmen started re-surfacing the sections which had been constructed out of Sainsbury's Homebase Readymix to save money.

So, it seemed, plus ça change. The Original Estimate Tablet of Giza seemed to provide irrefutable proof that the ancient Pharaohs were "stitched up" by their contractors, who took a century and a half to complete the Pyramids, doubtless with costs spiralling as they did so.

Here, then, was a clue to the fabulous wealth of the Masons, or their sinister brother organization, the Knights Templar. (The Templars are known to have virtually invented the modern banking system, and it may well be that they simply operated as the financial and military wings of the hugely powerful Masons.) For "masons" of course, we can read "builders", since, in the days before the introduction of pre-stressed concrete, "building" and "masonry" were synonymous. For, across the centuries, builders have controlled vast resources. The very image and renown of great empires rested on the building-skills of stonemasons. The Greeks built their great amphitheatres and the Parthenon. The Romans subdued Europe by constructing stone roads, forts, temples, and amazing feats of civil engineering such as Hadrian's Wall. Once emperors, kings or popes had accepted their estimates, and work had begun, the masons could proceed to suck them dry, adding cost-overruns and additional materials until the money gave out.

The Romans gave Europe aqueducts, cities and a road network, but bankrupted themselves in the process. The power of Ancient Egypt collapsed after the Pyramids project plunged it into massive debt. Gradually, builders, or masons, became the richest and most powerful group on Earth. Even today, in Britain, their power is such that no government minister, protest group or public enquiry can prevent them from doing whatever they want. To take but a small example, the Cleggan Field by-pass at Overton was granted planning permission despite being a protected area, a site of natural beauty, and regardless of a petition of over 3,000,000 signatures. Environment Minister Reginald Craven allowed the scheme to go ahead. Why? Was he visited in the night by strange men uttering terrible threats in unknown languages?

Moreover, it is surely unfeasible that, in centuries past, there were not major structural masterpieces built of wood – great ships, or bridges, or particularly elaborate examples of garden fencing. Yet wood-workers never became a vast, powerful clandestine secret society in the way that masons did. Why?

It was then I remembered that Jesus was a carpenter. A carpenter was an honest, simple tradesman, working with living wood. A stonemason was, then, the opposite – power-crazed, greedy, and bent on gaining vast wealth and holding the entire world in thrall. How did all this fit in with a time-share village in the South of France?

I looked on a map. The site of the time-share village was in the Languedoc, a mystical region, home of Catharism, the Merovingian kings, and the site of the Albigensian crusade, an event which it is obligatory to mention in books such as these. Could all these things be connected? I had no idea, but I knew that if had anything to do with it, they would be very soon.

CHAPTER TWO

The Conspiracy Deepens

This engraving, from 1493, clearly shows the dangers of drug-use at raves

As I continued my researches, I became aware that unknown forces were trying their best to prevent me from probing any deeper into this mystery. I received mysterious phone-calls in the evenings, often from people telling me that "a representative was in my area" and would I be interested in "new aluminium windows"? It seemed obvious to me that this was some kind of strange, coded warning not to interfere any further. I also began receiving alarming packages through the post. Frequently, these packages – which I had not ordered or requested – would entice me on the outside by informing me that I had 'Won £200,000', only to contain within a bewildering selection of leaflets, free-gift vouchers and requests to subscribe to magazines. It certainly seemed that some sort of dark forces were at work. Somehow they knew my address, and information about my family, often quoting my house-number in the letters.

I determined, however, to ignore this psychological harassment and continue my research. I had already formed the hypothesis that the Masons were the most powerful organization on Earth. It had also occurred to me that in the case of many stone-built masterpieces – such as Stonehenge, the Pyramids of Egypt and Mexico, and the Easter Island statues – scientists have never been able to work out how the ancient master-masons transported the huge blocks which were used. It had been suggested before that the Masons were, in fact, aliens, or, at least, got some help from alien levitational or anti-gravity techniques. This seemed a tantalizing possibility. It would also give me a link between the Masons and outer space, which I was sure my publishers would be very happy about.

None of this, however, explained the bizarre reference to Elvis Presley which had already come up in relation to the mystery. At first sight there seemed little possible connection between the pop icon and the vast power network of the Masons. But when I began to research more deeply I realised that I could not have been more wrong.

Firstly, Elvis's home was in Memphis, Tennessee: the original Memphis was a great city of Ancient Egypt! Furthermore, on one of his early hits, Elvis is clearly heard singing "Go, cat, go" – and the cat was the sacred animal of Ancient Egypt! Even more disturbingly, it is thought that the great slabs of rock which made up the Pyramids were transported by rolling them on logs. And Elvis Presley was the King of... "Rock and Roll!" It seemed too incredible to be true – that an entire strand of popular music could be named after a technique for setting vast stone slabs into position. If it *was* true, then it would indicate that, incredibly, pop music itself was nothing more than part of the complex Masonic plot to rule the world. Yet, wherever I looked, proof seemed to be staring me in the face. The word "Beatles", for example, is a pun on the word "Beetle" – and the scarab beetle was another sacred creature in Ancient Egypt! Furthermore, the Beatles' original name was... the Quarrymen! Even more unbelievably, the Beatles' chief rivals were... the Rolling Stones!

I had never before taken seriously the idea that pop music was part of a sinister conspiracy to control the minds of youth all over the world, but now, reluctantly, I was forced to consider that possibility. Furthermore, I was forced to come to grips with a conundrum that confronts all good conspiracy theorists: the assassination of John F. Kennedy in November, 1963.

CHAPTER THREE
The Conspiracy Clots

Of all the uncertainties and mysteries surrounding the assassination of JFK, there is only really one fact which anyone knows for certain – there's a lot of money been made out of it. This one fact was the only clue I had to go on when I began my extensive research into the subject, by going down to my local video shop and renting Oliver Stone's film. Oliver Stone, of course, also directed The Doors, a film about a rock group, and rock groups were already under deep suspicion, especially since doors are, of course, often used by builders – ostensibly to provide access between rooms, but perhaps for some other, deeper, reason.

Kennedy's White House had been known as "Camelot", a clear reference to the Arthurian myth. The Knights of Arthur had sought the Holy Grail – perhaps President Kennedy, too, had sought some kind of grail. But what kind? Of course, everyone knows that Kennedy had taken America into the Space Race with the USSR, promising that the United States would land a man on the moon before the decade was out. Did this declared aim alarm somebody? Did somebody have some reason for *not* wanting men to land on the moon? Perhaps they would find something there that they were not supposed to?

It was a tantalizing theory, and one for which there was no evidence whatsoever. But that very lack of evidence indicated a massive cover-up. I had recently discovered a valuable document in a junk-shop. The proprietor, evidently failing to realise its true value, had placed it in a box marked "Everything 10p!" Much to my amazement, I found that one of the items he considered only worth 10p was none other than Giles Valois-Exentrique's renowned work, *Aliens Killed Kennedy by Mind Control.*

One of the most-discussed aspects of the Kennedy affair is that fact that no-one actually saw the gunman. Why? The answer is simple – because the gunman was an alien capable of becoming invisible to the human eye. It seems so simple, yet no-one has publicly discussed this possibility. Why? Because it is "plainly the ravings of a nutter". That is always the argument put forward by the Establishment to discredit any theories which they find uncomfortable, or which threaten to expose their sinister conspiracies.

In the Warren Commission Report on the presidential assassination, not one mention is made of the possibility that Kennedy's assassin was an alien from another galaxy. Why? Clearly someone, somewhere, had something to hide. Mr Joe Brindley, an unemployed psychic researcher from Wacksville, Idaho, requested fourteen times that the Warren Commission hear his testimony. The flimsy excuse offered by the Commission was that Mr Brindley was clearly "a total fruitcake" who would "waste valuable time". This is yet more evidence of the familiar tactic of the Establishment forces – to discredit those who seek to expose them by implying that they are in some way not compos mentis.

Had the Commission spoken to Mr Brindley, they might have concluded that President Kennedy was not killed by Lee Harvey Oswald but by a Terminator Series T-1000 from the future. Kennedy's space programme undoubtedly led to major technological advances – such as the Teflon frying pan – which would not have been made had Kennedy not funded space research. It could be that the Space Race was leading to the building of a supercomputer which would eventually develop an independent intelligence, begin replicating itself, and eventually wipe out humanity. The fictional "Terminator" films starring Arnold Schwarzenegger might well have been made as a teasing clue as to what really happened. This would indicate that all of Hollywood was part of the brain-washing propaganda machine, designed to keep the human race under the sinister control of the Freemasons.

This brought me back to Elvis Presley once more. After two years of unprecedented world superstardom as a rock'n'roll singer, Elvis disappeared into the Army and went to Germany. Why? Was he – as I suspected – an agent of the Masons? And why Germany? I had heard rumours from a reliable source that, in the last days of the Nazis, vast amounts of gold, treasure and possibly even the Lost Ark of the Covenant were placed in safe storage to keep them out of the hands of the advancing Allies.

Where were those treasures now? Had they, as my source suggested, been buried beneath the new Autobahn network where no-one would think to look for them? This theory only seemed to be confirmed when my source suddenly died, in mysterious circumstances. He was found in a ditch, and an autopsy revealed "enormous amounts of alcohol" in his blood, indicating that he had been "pissed as a newt" and that, furthermore, "he was lucky this hadn't happened before". Who had wanted him dead badly enough to buy him that many drinks? Could it be the sinister Masonic conspiracy? How had they known about him? In all the years I had known him, I never saw him outside the Saloon Bar in the Pig and Ferret. How had they found out about him?

Whatever the truth, the undeniable fact was that, when Elvis Presley came out of the Army, he suddenly began making films, and most of them were mindnumbingly bad. Why did he do it? Could it be that this was merely a cover? For Elvis had now spent two years in the Army, learning, amongst other things, how to load, clean and fire a range of weapons. Could it be that Elvis was taken to Germany to train to assassinate Kennedy? No policeman would ever suspect the multi-millionaire pop idol, and the staff at the National Book Depository on Dealey Plaza would have been delighted to let him in, almost certainly without any security checks. Elvis was the perfect assassin. It would also explain the persistent rumours that Elvis was himself murdered in 1977. He simply knew too much.

But none of this explained the death of Marilyn Monroe a year earlier. I had long been interested in her mysterious demise, chiefly because there were so many books about it that my local bookshop had started a special "Marilyn Monroe" section, which was slightly larger than the rest of the Non-Fiction department. Evidently it was necessary to consider how her death fitted in with the jigsaw that was beginning to build up. Both the CIA and the Mafia had been implicated, but no-one seemed to have considered the Freemasons. Yet, if Elvis Presley had been brainwashed by Masonic agents into killing Kennedy, and Marilyn had found out about it, this might well explain why she "seemed worried" at the time of her death.

CHAPTER FOUR
The Conspiracy Goes a Bit Lumpy

I was now faced with the possibility that the Freemasons were the direct descendents of aliens who landed in Egypt, and passed their knowledge down through obscure Rosicrucian sects who would never reveal themselves openly, because that would be too obvious or something. Instead, they worked behind the scenes of history.

Galileo, for example, is said to have begun his researches after receiving an anonymous note reading, "Suppose we went round the sun? Just a thought." Sir Isaac Newton was once approached by a hooded figure in a street who simply whispered, "Go and sit under that tree," and sidled away.

Similarly, there is a mysterious Huguenot sect who seem to have been operative in Paris just before the French Revolution. Calling themselves the Secte Mysterieuse Huguenot, their role in founding the first post-monarchical society and paving the way for the modern world is unclear, but I reckon they did. It cannot simply have been coincidence.

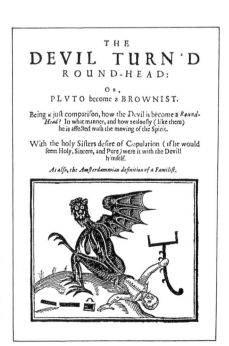

THE
DEVIL TURN'D
ROUND-HEAD:
OR,
PLVTO become a BROWNIST.

Being a just comparison, how the Devil is become a Round-Head? In what manner, and how zealously (like them) he is affected with the moving of the Spirit.

With the holy Sisters desire of Copulation (if he would seem Holy, Sincere, and Pure) were it with the Devill himself.

As also, the Amsterdammian definition of a Familist.

One of the objective, level-headed source books I used in my research

Then there is the mysterious figure of Rasputin, the strange bearded monk who did so much to discredit the Russian monarchy prior to the Revolution. Why did Rasputin wear a monk's hood? Why did he have a beard? Could it have been because he was not actually human? And why were they able to shoot him and poison him and he still didn't die? Was he, in fact, a robot from the future? Or were they just crap shots?

If this hypothesis is true – and I believe that it is – then it seemed obvious to me that the Masons – in the guise of their contemporary counterparts, Builders – were responsible for the time-share fiasco in the South of France which my prodcuer had so fatally investigated. Perhaps these small-time cons are just fringe activities, to raise money to fund the vast central project of Freemasonry.

What this project is, I am not yet sure, although it may be that they plan to install a giant atomic engine at the earth's core and steer our planet away to a far-distant galaxy to replace their own planet which was lost in an asteroid storm. This may seem a far-fetched scenario but the Dutch Renaissance hermetic mystic, philosopher-poet Hans-Franke Stratejaket, in his 1598 pamphlet *De Planno Secreto de Templii*, predicted with uncanny accuracy the assassination of Kennedy, the date of World War II, and the missing of a penalty by Stuart Pearce in a World Cup semi-final in 1990. Given the amazingly accurate nature of these predictions, coupled with his correspondence with John Dee (which he must have had, surely), who can say whether his final prediction, that the Templars' plan – "orbum mondo spaceshippo fecit" – is incorrect?

I am also convinced that Jesus knew of this scheme, objected to it, and was subsequently abducted in a spaceship and taken away, to be held prisoner on Planet Torb.

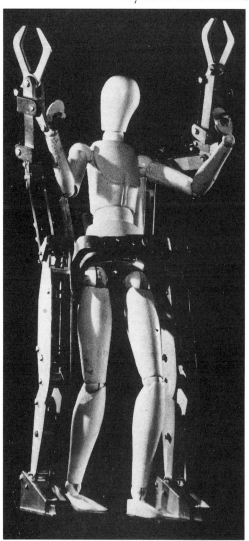

Did cyborg robo-slaves build the pyramids? It would explain a lot

I hope to find evidence of this, although the massed forces of the Vatican Establishment have already, through their puppets in the media, labelled me "another utter mentler".

90

NOTES ON SOURCES

(1)   *The Wholly Mad and the Holy Grail (London, 1982), p.45.*

(2)   *Les Secretes Grands des Pharaohs (Paris, La Presse Loony, 1965), p.456.*

(3)   *Bow Low to the Parsnip: A Treatise upon the Divers Profane and Idolatrous Practices of the Brotherhood of Worshipful Greengrocers (London, Simpserson & Boddle, 1689).*

(4)   *Better Gardening the Rosicrucian Way (London, Oddball Press, 1976).*

(5)   *Assassins of Atlantis: Proof that Aliens have Infiltrated the CIA!! (New York, Bonkers & Bonkers Ltd., 1984).*

(6)   *Thou Art Translated: Cabbalistic Alchemy and the Symbolism of Metempsychosis in A Midsummer Night's Dream (Article in Obscure and Tedious Literary Quarterly, Vol. XXVII, Cambridge University Press, 1952).*

(7)   *Ibid., p.47.*

(8)   *From "Build Your Own Sacrificial Altar", Blue Peter Annual 1976 (London, BBC Publications).*

(9)   *The Yoghurt of the Nile: Conclusive Proof that the Ancient Egyptians Invented the Refrigerator in 950 BC (Los Angeles, Wacko Press, 1987).*

(10) *The Doctrines of the Knights Templar and their Influence on Coronation Street, 1960-92 (Article in Frankly Off-Their-Rocker Review, Vol.26, pp.78-96. OUP, 1993).*

(11) *Ibid., p.23.*

(12) *They Said I Was Mad!!! Memoirs of King Richard the Second by Tony Gruntham (London, Eccentric Press, 1991).*

(13) *The Mafia Had Eldorado Taken Off (London, Yentob and Powell, 1993).*

(14) *Play Better Football the Beelzebub Way (with an Introduction by Vinny Jones) (London, Hill & Venables, 1992).*

CINEMA

"The indispensible
guide to late-night
movie-watching."

the
Post-
Pub

FILM
GUIDE

ERIC DENTON

3rd Edition

Every night since his fifteenth birthday, Eric Denton has got tanked up at his local pub, come home, eaten whatever happened to be in the fridge, and flopped down on the sofa to watch a film. He now uses the unique insight he has gained into the world of motion pictures to bring us *The Post-Pub Film Guide*. In his drunken stupor he has started to watch over 9,500 movies. Unfortunately the *Guide* is restricted to the 25 or so through which he has managed to remain conscious.

His other publications include *The Post-Pub Guide to Finding Your Own House, The Post-Pub Guide to Breakfast Cereal* (Fifth Edition), and *The Spinning Room*, an autobiographical account of his many post-pub experiences.

Eric Denton is 22 and has a beer gut the size of a basketball.

What the critics said:

"For lads, *Denton's Film Guide* is now more invaluable than ever. No other guide tells you where the rude bits are, so you can Fast Forward on your video." *Bazzer, Essex*

"With its emphasis on the films lads actually want to see: those with tits, shagging and mindless violence, *Denton's Film Guide* is an essential companion." *Vince,"The Dog and Duck", Romford*

Blues Brothers

US 1980 133m Technicolor
Universal

This is popular with bloody students and that. It's a sort of cult film and they put it on with that other load of bollocks, what's it called?... *Brazil*, that's it. It's got loads of old fashioned music in it. I don't get the point of it. Tell you what I did like, though. That *Blue Thunder* thing about the helicopter in LA that pumps criminals with a Kalashnikov thing that's strapped to it. That's the business.

w Dan Ackroyd, John Landis d John Landis

John Belushi, Dan Ackroyd, James Brown

Brazil

GB 1985 142m colour
Embassy

All set in the future or something. Bleeding complicated when you're pissed. Anyway, they always put it on at the cinema with that *Blue Thunder* thing, about John Belushi and Aretha Franklin as two helicopter pilots.

w Terry Gilliam, Tom Stoppard d Terry Gilliam

Jonathan Price, Bob Hoskins, Robert de Niro

Casablanca *

US 1942 102m bw
Warner

Really famous and really rubbish. It's all in black and white for a start. There's a wine bar near me called Casablanca, with loads of pictures of Humphrey Bogart on the walls. I don't go there because they don't have beer. Wankers. Anyway, this film is meant to have loads of sublimated sexual desire in it. So what. Where's the nobbing?

w Julius J. Epstein, Howard Koch
d Michael Curtiz

Humphrey Bogart, Ingrid Bergmann, Claude Rains, Peter Lorré, Dooley Wilson, Paul Heinreid

Dances With Wolves

US 1992 too bloody long colour

Too bleeding long, but the girl looks fit in all that Indian squaw stuff. To be honest, I fell asleep in the middle for about 20 minutes, but all I missed was one shot of the landscape. Didn't like it to start with because I kept on thinking that bastard Steve Bull would pop up. Goal-Sitting Bull I call him. haaaa.

wd Kevin Costner p Kevin Costner

Kevin Costner, loads of Indians

Draughtsman's Contract, The

GB 1982 108m colour

Piss off.

wd Some ponce

Some other ponce, and a posh bird

ET **

US 1982 115m De Luxe
Universal

Spaceship crashes on earth and one of its occupants takes refuge with an American family. This was the highest grossing box office film in history. You're supposed to cry at the end but I didn't. Everyone else in the room did, but I didn't. I've never cried over anything, except when Arsenal lost the League championship. Anyway, why should you cry over a little rubber alien that looks

95

like Paul Daniels? And all that "Phone home" bollocks. If he's so bleeding advanced why can't he do it by telepathy or something?

w Melissa Mathieson d Steven Spielberg m John Williams

Drew Barrymore, Dee Wallace

Fantasia

US 1940 135m Technicolor

Got it out the video shop 'cos it sounded a bit porny. Turned out to be classical music and cartoons of under the sea and bollocks like that. Written by someone who's had too many drugs and stuff I reckon, or maybe a friend of that Dustin Hoffman (See *Tootsie*, or rather, don't!)

w Some nutter d Mr Bleeding Cheesecake, if you ask me

Gone With The Wind

US 1939 220m Technicolor

A real bum-breaker. It was only halfway through when I lost all the feeling in me arse. Had to get up and go for a stagger into the kitchen to get another beer. At the end I always want Clark Gable to say "Frankly, my dear, I don't give a flying pig's fart," but he never does.

Good Fellas

US 1990 123m colour
Universal

Bobby de Niro does a bloke in the back of a car. He's a bloody psychopath. Magic. And little Pesci. "You think I'm a funny guy? How funny? Funny how? Funny haha? You laugh? You laugh because I am funny?" There's a bloke at the pub like that. Come to think of it, it's me.

wd Martin Scorcese

Robert de Niro, Joe Pesci, Ray Liotta

Great Escape, The

US 1963 173m De Luxe/Panavision

It's always on at Christmas, this one. It's the one about the blokes who escape from the prisoner of war camp. It's quite good actually, but then I'm always pissed and full of mince pies when I see it. As for that "Good Luck", "Thank you" bit – stupid bloody wanker. No wonder he ended up on *Upstairs Downstairs*. Mind you, he was in *The Professionals*. That was good.

w James Clavell d John Sturges

Steve McQueen, James Garner, Dickie Bleeding Attenborough, Gordon Jackson

Jaws ***

US 1975 125m Technicolor
Universal

Lots of blood, but the shark is made of bleeding rubber. Didn't scare me.

w Peter Benchley d Steven Spielberg

Robert Shaw, Roy Scheider (he's in that Blue Thunder thing), Richard Dreyfuss

Kick Boxer ****

US 1992 100m

Now you're talking. This has got that Jean Claude Van Damme bloke in it. Basically the film starts, and then he beats people shitless for an hour and a half. Doesn't matter what they've done. Just looked at him a bit funny maybe. He doesn't care. Just beats them shitless, or smashes their heads against a brick wall or something. Magic.

w Didn't need one d Who cares?

Jean Claude Van Damme, lots of big blokes who don't mind being beaten shitless

Lethal Weapon

US 1987 110m Technicolor
Warner

My bird fancies that Mel Gibson, but I think he's a git.

w Shane Black d Richard Donner

Mel Gibson (bastard)

Manhattan

US 1979 96m bw Panavision

That Woody Allen, eh. In this he's trying to get off with a 17-year-old. Too old for him, if you ask me. Huuur huuur huuur. This won an Oscar, I think. Tell you what, it wasn't for tits. You don't see any of them. Not even a flash. Probably because it's low budget. The whole thing's in black and white for a start. I preferred *Porky's*, which is sort of the same but different.

wd Woody Allen p Gordon Willis

Woody Allen, Diane Keaton, Meryl Streep, Mariel Hemingway (huuur)

No Way Out

US 1988 112m colour
Paramount

Kevin Costner gets off with this bird in the back of a limo after about ten minutes. You

might as well switch it off after that.

w Buggered if I know

d I'd have done it for the first ten minutes

Kevin Costner, Sean Young

Psycho

US 1960 109m bw
Shamley/Alfred Hitchcock

This is by that Alfred Hitchcock. He was fat. This bloke kills this bird in a shower. Sometimes I feel like doing that to mine, especially when she's in there and the door's locked and I'm busting for a piss. Anyway this bloke has killed his Mum. Hang on, I did that too. And then he goes round wearing her dress. No way. No bleeding way! That is not normal.

w Joseph Stefano d Alfred Hitchcock

Anthony Perkins, Janet Leigh

Return Of The Mad Mechanoid Machete Monks *****

GB 1993 23m
My mate Ron

This is totally bleeding brilliant but not many people have seen it 'cos it was made by my mate Ron in his garage, and on location in the woods up by his house. At the moment he's having a bit of a problem distributing it, 'cos he's run out of cassettes. Plus the police are after him 'cos of some of the things in it. I told him he should put it in for Cannes and that 'cos the French must be fed up with all that ponce by now, and are probably aching to see a medieval holy man get his bonce lopped off with a machete, and watch all his innards go everywhere.

He said they would probably need a plot, but I told him French films never have one anyway. I saw that *Jean de Florette*. It was bollocks.

wd My mate Ron

Ron, Dave, Vince and his Missus, Spikey, Lord Justice Wallaby

Some Like It Hot

US 1959 122m bw
UA/Mirisch

That Marilyn Monroe, eh. I wouldn't kick her out of bed for eating crisps. I wouldn't kick anyone out of bed for eating crisps, because I always eat crisps in bed. Anyway, Marilyn, she got knocked off by Kennedy apparently, and then got wasted by the CIA or the Mafia or something. Pity the film's not about that really. It's about two blokes who dress up as birds. You wouldn't catch me doing that. Not for no-one. Do you hear me? Not for no-one! Bloody weirdos!

w Billy Wilder (Billy Weirder, know what I mean?)

d Billy Wilder m Adolph Deutsch

Jack Lemmon, Tony Curtis, Marilyn Monroe

Star Wars *

US 1977 121m Technicolor/Panavision
TCF/Lucas Film

This simply plotted but special-effects-laden bonanza proved a smash hit at the box office, is what it said in the *TV Times*, but they know dick-all. Basically it's got those robots in it, and that Carrie Fisher. I mean, you'd give her one. And that Harrison Ford. My bird fancies him, but I don't think he's

got anything I haven't. In fact I've got quite a lot he hasn't. A huge gut, for example. Anyway, it all gets soppy at the end. And there's not enough blood.

wd George Lucas m John Williams pd John Barry

Harrison Ford, Carrie Fisher, Peter Cushing, Alec Guinness and that Darth Vader bloke

Terminator ****

US 1990 Not long enough
Warner

Arnie is a killing machine. Literally. He's a bloody robot thing that kills people. And nothing can stop him. He blows people's heads off, and you see everything. Brilliant.

wd probably Arnie, I should think

Arnie, some bird

Tootsie

US 1982 116m colour
Columbia/Mirage

That Dustin Hoffman. He was good in *Marathon Man*, but in this he's a bleeding transvestite, just like Tony Curtis, Jack Lemmon and that Anthony Perkins geezer. Horrible. They're probably all members of the Hollywood Trannies Club. Ponce about each other's pools dressed in bikinis and that. You wouldn't get Van Damme in a dress. If you suggested it to him, he'd beat you shitless.

w Larry Gelbart

d Sydney Pollack (Sydney. Funny name. See what I mean?)

Dustin Hoffman, Jessica Lange (Whoooah)

Top Gun

US 1986 116m Metrocolor
Paramount

Fighter pilots, alright! Fighter pilots pulling top class birds, alright! I wanted to be a fighter pilot but I was too fat. And too stupid. "There's a MIG on your tail, Eric, er... Red Leader... OK I've got him... got to get a lock... got to get a lock... locked... release missile... boom". Dead Red in Indian Ocean. Pity the Cold War's over, innit? Kelly McGillis is in it, but you don't see nothing. Not like in *Witness*, eh.

w Jim Cash d Tony Scott

Tom Cruise, Kelly McGillis, Val Kilmer (he's married to that Joanne Whalley. Lucky bastard)

Total Recall ****

US 1988 123m colour
Warner

Arnie gets reprogrammed to be a killing machine (what was he before, then? A bleeding flower arranger?) and blows loads of people away. I watched that *Kindergarten Cop*, and he didn't waste anyone. What's the point of that then?

w Who needs them? Arnie does it on instinct

d I told you. It's instinctive. Arnie is a killing machine. They just film him doing it.

Arnie, some other bird

When Harry Met Sally

US 1991 123m Colour

Bleeding soppy. Meant to be funny but it didn't make me laugh. There's this bit where this bird embarrasses this bloke in a cafe by faking an orgasm. No bird has ever done that to me. Come to think of it no bird has ever had a real one with me either.

wd Can't remember - too pissed p Same, sorry

Meg Ryan, Billy Crystal (what sort of a name is that? He'd probably put on a dress if you asked him to)

"Fascinating, riveting, occasionally gruesome. Fully illustrated, including a putrid corpse and a binbag with some limbs in it."

A NICE SIT-DOWN
WITH SOME
HORRIFIC
MURDERERS

COLIN FEYDEAU

FOREWORD

"Murder most Foul..."

WILLIAM SHAKESPEARE

Why are we so fascinated by murder? Ever since Thomas de Quincey wrote "Murder Considered as one of the Fine Arts", the subject of murder has been a respectable one; many fine, upstanding citizens, who would not harm a fly, are nevertheless enthralled by tales of how human beings set about eliminating each other. Whether we are dealing with a Victorian poisoner, or a modern-day serial killer, two things remain constant: our morbid curiosity and our insatiable appetite for true crime.

For true crime has one major advantage over fictional crime. Fictional crime always places the emphasis on the motive. In fiction, a murderer always has a simple, readily understandable motive. In contemporary crime-writing, this may be something psychological, but it will still be simple and easily isolated. In Agatha Christie, of course, it will be something moronically simple – a valuable brooch, or a bequest in a will, or some such crap. These externalized motives make us feel comfortable, and provide the rounded sense of narrative that fiction requires.

What makes true crime so much more exciting is that, frequently, real-life murderers do not have such cut-and-dried motives. They are just crazy apeshit-bonkers psycho maniacs. Be scared. Be very scared. They're out there. Nor does true crime waste time giving you lots of false clues and possible suspects. It goes right to the heart of the matter and tells you all the gory details you want to know, and often you get a picture too.

So, following the success of my previous books *Browse Through Some Slayings* and *A Home Compendium of Mass Killers*, I am delighted to set down the true stories of a few more psychotic nutters, which should please readers and publisher alike. Settle back, then, and enjoy *A Nice Sit-Down With Some Horrific Murderers*.

C. FEYDEAU : CELL 14B, PARKHURST

THE STUPID KILLER

In 1954, South London was terrorized by a series of murders carried out by an assailant whom the press swiftly dubbed the "Stupid Killer" or "Remedial Ripper". The murders were characterized by clues so obvious, and mistakes so crass, that for months police believed that it had to be a blind, a deliberate attempt to lead them down a false trail.

Unfortunately, it turned out that, in fact, the killer was just very thick, and in the meantime the police had let him get away with many more murders.

The first victim was Donald Dudgeon, a newsagent from Tulse Hill, who was just about to close up his shop one day when a man came in wanting to arrange newspaper delivery to his house. He gave his name as Jack "Mad Axe" Morgan, and his address as Mad Axe Cottage, Lower Nevis Drive, Croydon. As Mr Dudgeon was writing this down in his delivery book, Morgan killed him with a large axe, which he had purchased two minutes earlier from the hardware shop next door. He then fled, leaving the axe and his wallet.

Police suspicion immediately fell on Rodney Rumney, a known violent criminal with a record of serious assaults. Rumney was now 89, half-blind and serving a ten-year sentence in Wandsworth Prison, but detectives calculated that he could have broken out of his cell, scaled the wall, stolen a guide dog, and made his way to Tulse Hill in time for the killing, afterwards heading to a lock-up garage containing his getaway wheelchair. But before Rumney could be questioned, the killer struck again, this time in the middle of Norwood High Street in broad daylight. He strangled Mrs Dorothy Watkiss, a 56-year old mother-of-four, outside Dawson the Butcher's. As she slumped lifeless to the pavement, Morgan turned to the crowd of assembled onlookers and said, "Thank you very much. My name is Jack 'Mad Axe' Morgan. If you have any irritating relatives, ex-partners or business associates you would like me to brutally murder, please get in touch." He then gave his daytime phone number.

The Thaxted Throttler (see previous page)

The police were baffled. The first thing they needed to do was find Jack's real identity. Word went out through their South London contact network that anyone who knew "Mad Axe's" real name could be in for a substantial reward if they informed on him. A day later they were phoned by the parish vicar of St Mary's, Pollompton, Dorset. In the parish christening records was a Jack Anthony Peregrine Mad Axe Morgan, born 1906. His mother's name was Annie Jocelyn Piano-Wire Trudgewell, his father's name, Ronald Spencer Blunt Instrument Morgan.

Now police knew that they had a clever killer on their hands. Anyone who would go to the trouble of forging parish documents to establish their alias was evidently a very clever criminal indeed. Police began searching for someone very clever, suspicion first falling on Vladimir Popyov, a young Russian chess-player. But he was able satisfactorily to prove that he was in Minsk at the time of the Norwood slaying. Sir Michael Danby, Senior Research Fellow in Astrophysics at Cambridge, was also questioned. But although he was, indeed, very clever, police could not break his alibi.

Now Jack felt bolder. Two days later he broke into the home of Sid and Norma Trevis of Kennington and strangled them both with his tie. Police found the tie at the scene of the crime. On the back was a sewn-on name-tape reading J.M.A. Morgan. J.M.A Morgan was, by coincidence, also the name of a highly regarded author, writer of several award-winning novels including *Muffins At Noon*, *A Frightful State of Affairs*, and

103

Penistone's Socks. Police dragged him from his home in Shepton Mallet and interrogated him for three days. At the time of the first two killings, he had been staying with the playwright "Pinky" Pinkerton – author of *The Day the Croquet Stopped* – at his home in Cap d'Antibes, in the South of France. But when the stranglings had taken place in Kennington, Morgan had been only three miles away in Mayfair, attending a literary luncheon at the Cafe Royal. Other guests told the police that, around the time of the stranglings, Morgan had "popped out to the toilet" and been absent for at least four minutes. This, police calculated, was ample time to have flown across the Thames on some sort of rocket-propelled jet-pack, done the murders, and returned to the Cafe Royal.

It seemed that Morgan would face the gallows until Jack killed again while Morgan was still in police custody.

This time, Mad Axe made a fatal mistake – he strangled a man in broad daylight right in front of a passing policeman. The policeman, seeing the strangling going on, caught Mad Axe red-handed and proceeded to question him. When asked why he had strangled someone to death in the middle of the street, Morgan panicked and claimed that the man was actually an alien, whom he had strangled in order to prevent him taking over the Earth by mind control. The policeman agreed with Mad Axe that this was a terrifying prospect, and congratulated him on his quick action. "We'd just be the slaves of a race of beings from another world if it weren't for quick-thinking chaps like yourself," he told him. "Mind how you go, sir."

Still further emboldened, Mad Axe Morgan now sent invitations to local police officers, lawyers, and journalists, inviting them to attend the next murder, which, he said, would be held At Home at 7.30pm the following Thursday.

Dismissing the invitations as the work of an obvious crank, none of the invited guests turned up, leaving Mad Axe very angry, as he had a large number of sandwiches and crisps going completely to waste. The intended victim, Mr Barry Crumble, helped him to eat them, and Morgan then dismembered him with a machete. Whilst he was doing this, one of the journalists did actually turn up, but no-one answered the door. "The screaming and yelling from inside the house was so loud, they couldn't hear the bell," he later told police, "so I went to the pub." Half an hour later he was surprised to see a man walk into the pub covered in blood and carrying a large machete. When he asked the man about this, he was told, "I've just killed someone in cold blood." The journalist laughed, and Morgan promptly severed his right leg with the machete, and then proceeded to kill everyone in the pub. He then sat and waited for the police to arrive. When they did, he killed them all.

With this final gesture – the killing of 37 innocent people in the same night – Mad Axe Morgan decided that he'd had enough. He never killed again. He gave himself up, and when the police refused to believe his story, he passed sentence on himself and, after failing to get any prison to take him, he proceeded to incarcerate himself by building a brick wall around himself and staying in it for 20 years. He later become convinced that his conviction was unsafe, and is now planning an appeal.

THE KILLER SOLICITOR

Alfred Willard Chartwell had a childhood ambition to become a famous criminal barrister, and dreams of becoming a judge. However, whilst studying Law at university it became apparent that he was not temperamentally suited to this side of the profession. "He would attend lectures on Criminal Law relating to Murder," recalled one of his tutors, "and sit at the back, drooling, muttering and, instead of taking notes, drawing small pictures of the devil."

In his final exam for his law degree, he wrote an 11-page essay on the subject of "Evidential Procedural Reform in Relation to Capital Punishment". The essay consisted of the single word "Die" written 3,465 times in red ink; he passed with a 2:1. After Oxford, he went to Law school in London.

However, it was decided that it might be better if Chartwell practised some area of law not directly related to murder, and he became a solicitor specializing in house conveyancing and searches prior to purchase. In 1952, he joined a practice in the sleepy village of Gummersham, West Surrey, and did well, becoming a partner at the age of 33.

The firm was now known as Wintlesham, Popkiss and Chartwell, but just six months later, Chartwell suddenly had a new nameplate made reading Wintlesham, Popkiss and The Avenger. He told Mr Wintlesham (who dealt with wills) that he wanted to "wipe the scum from the face of West Surrey". Quite what this meant no-one realised until Mrs Ena Grant, who was trying to buy a house in West Clandon, discovered that the prospective seller had failed to inform her of severe damp in the basement. On consulting her solicitor, Alfred Chartwell, she was told that he would "deal with it". Two days later the vendor was discovered severed in two with a machete. The only clue was a note sent to Mrs Grant the following day, which read:

The Suffolk
Suffolkator
(see p. 173)

FEE

In the matter of disposing of the Scumbag in West Clandon   £30

Incidental Expenses incurred, viz.

Purchase of Machete   £4.10s.6d

Dry-Cleaning   6s 4d

Various Disbursements   £2.5s.0d

£37.1s.10d

YOUR PROMPT SETTLEMENT WOULD BE APPRECIATED

Forensic tests on the note revealed no fingerprints or other evidence, although police came to the conclusion that the note must be a hoax, largely because the charge for the "various disbursements" was far too reasonable a sum to have been the work of a real solicitor.

Meanwhile, Mr Chartwell was conducting a title-search for another client, a Mr Ronald Spade of Wilmsleigh, who was attempting to buy a house in Chittingstone from a man called Willard. When Chartwell consulted the Property Register he discovered that it was not Willard's to sell; it belonged to his great-aunt, who had died ten years earlier, and was part of a contested will. Had Mr Spade bought it, Willard would have taken the money and fled, leaving Spade with no rights on the property and no way of reclaiming his money. Alfred wrote a letter to his client, to the effect that "in view of the failure to disclose the Charge on the property, it is my considered opinion that you should Withdraw from the purchase, and that furthermore and moreover, in this matter it would be advisable if I Blew this Miserable Ratfink Scumbag away he must DIE he will

DIE yes he is DEAD YES HE IS A DEAD MAN KILL KILL KILL oh yesohyesohyes HE is DEAD BYE BYE DEAD. Please advise as to your approval of this proposed course of action. Yours, The Avenger."

When Mr Spade wrote back, saying that he felt that he would prefer to instigate a civil action to recover his deposit, Chartwell sent the following by return:

FEE

In the matter of wiping out human filth Willard   £30 ____

Incidental Expenses incurred, viz.   ____

Purchase of "Mauser" sub-machine gun   £125 ____

Purchase of 200 rounds steel-tipped bullets £26. 6s 3d

Various Disbursements £26. 7s

Total   £204. 13s 3d

YOUR PROMPT SETTLEMENT WOULD BE APPRECIATED

By now, suspicions were being voiced about Chartwell. He had recently discovered that a house being purchased by one of his clients was on the likely route of a new main road, which would remove almost twenty yards of the front garden. The vendor had never mentioned this. "In view of the failure to inform us of this Planning Application," Chartwell wrote to his client, "it is, in my opinion, essential to slice out this man's liver, and then eat it with fava beans and a nice Chianti." This he did, and when a man in Guildford gazumped one of Chartwell's clients a week later, Chartwell threw him under a train.

Police now arrested the crazed solicitor, who told them he was "on a mission to rid the world of those who would not adopt honourable practices in property transaction". When word of this leaked to the Press, Chartwell unexpectedly became a popular hero. "AT LAST! A REAL MAN-IAC!" blazoned one headline, whilst the *Daily Bulletin* began a "Save Our Loony" campaign: "At last – a legal-eagle who actually shows his talons!" read one editorial. "Plucky Alf Chartwell, 38, doesn't mess about with all that namby-pamby, longwinded nonsense that the wallies in wigs usually give us. When someone tries to rip off one of Alf's clients, he rips off their head! We say – three cheers for Alf!"

The Chelmsford Choker (see p. 213)

"DOT" WATLEY

In one of the most notorious cases of recent years, Mrs Dorothy Watley of Exeter, Devon, was given a life sentence for murdering three husbands in a row, each time for the life insurance. In each case all the circumstantial evidence pointed to Mrs Watley, and the motive was clearly established, but, for more than five years, police were totally baffled as to the method by which the men were murdered. It was only through the brilliant detective work of Mr John Massington of the Scotland Yard Murder Squad that, eventually, Mrs Watley's almost foolproof technique was discovered. Three times, she had bored husbands to death by reading to them from political memoirs.

The first victim, Alan Plaxted, was a heating engineer who married Watley in June 1988. Only two weeks later, his bride went into Grassley's Bookshop and bought a copy of *Ministers Decide* by Norman Fowler. Three days later, Alan Plaxted was dead. The post-mortem revealed "a state of total catatonic seizure". His body was "rigid, eyes staring, face contorted in an agony of total uninterest" while his brain, according to the pathologist Martin Simons, had "atrophied into a blank mass".

The next victim, Ronnie Garrold, worked for a local carpet-fitting company. He married Dorothy in May 1990. In early July, his new wife joined the Remainder Book Club through an advert in a Sunday colour supplement, and her first purchase was a copy of *A Sparrow's Flight:Memoirs of Lord Hailsham*. Garrold was dead within a week, his symptoms similar to Plaxted's: death in unimaginable agony. Police suspicions began to be aroused, but they could prove nothing.

Now Dorothy seemed to get bolder. When the newspapers announced the publication of David Owen's *Time To Declare*, she decided it was time to marry again. However, this time, she ran into problems. Her third husband, Timothy Norris, was an ex-Social Democrat supporter who already actually owned a copy of the *A Life at the Centre* by Roy Jenkins. To his wife's shock and disbelief, he rather enjoyed her nightly readings from *Time To Declare*, once making a point of saying that the sections about Owen's doubts concerning the Labour Party during the period of the Lib-Lab pact were "really rather fascinating". Clearly, Dorothy was in trouble, and her resolve hardened. There was only one solution – a copy of *An American Life* by Ronald Reagan. But even this failed to work on Norris, who, Rasputin-like, emerged every morning from his stupor still breathing and still very much alive. Desperate now, Dorothy resorted to desperate measures, buying memoirs by Geoffrey Howe, Cecil Parkinson, and even a life of Chancellor Kohl, which put Norris into a temporary coma, from which he recovered after a fortnight.

Finally, in despair, Dorothy was wandering around WH Smith in Plymouth when she suddenly found a copy of *Margaret Thatcher: The Woman Within*. This notorious volume, used by the Thaxted Strangler to anaesthetize his victims while he bundled them into his van, had Norris dead of acute boredom within three short days.

This time, police were ahead of Watley. Tracing her book-club purchases, they had anticipated her intention, and secretly bugged her bedroom. The resulting tape, played in court, had the jury ashen-faced at her cruelty and callousness. She was sentenced to life imprisonment, with a recommendation from Lord Justice Codger that she serve not less than 200 years. As she was dragged from the courtroom, she shouted at the judge that, "one day John Patten will write his memoirs and I'll come and read them to you".

"Lefty" Morelli, arriving at the Gang Boss of the Year Awards, 1924

"LEFTY" MORELLI

In the 1920s, a series of gang wars erupted between the Morelli family and everyone else. Father Morelli had emigrated from Sicily to New York in 1902, having seen his own mother killed by a local gang-boss for "putting too much parmesan on his spaghetti vongole". After "Studs" Vinelli wasted "Two-Shoes" Spinetti following the 4th Street Heist, "Trousers" Fantoni rubbed out the Bonetti twins for muscling in on "Switchblade" Martini's action on the Lower West Side. Ta-Ta Tantini, who had whacked Joey "The Horse" Bombini for singing to the Feds over Studs' racket, was wasted by the Nanini Brothers, while "Spats" Fanelli plugged "Robert de Niro Impression" Ranelli, leaving "Lefty" Morelli in a spot. Nobody was showing him any respect, and a man's gotta have respect. It grieved him, but it was regrettably necessary that he rub out the Fatman, who, his nose in the Corelli family had told him, was planning to join forces with the Barinis, waste "Spats" Fanelli and control the numbers on the Lower East Side. This he could not allow to happen.

On the evening of October 6th, 1925, "Lefty" gave orders to whack the Fatman, waste the Nanini Brothers, and personally beat "Ho-Ho" Dorelli to death with a pepper-grinder in Il Maniaco's restaurant. "Lefty" was arrested, but after half an hour, he was released by Police Lieutenant Harry O'Flagon because "there is not a shred of evidence against this upstanding citizen".

O'Flagon left his one-room apartment the next day and moved to Bermuda, where he bought a yacht and 200 acres.

TERMINATOR, THE

A bizarre trial in Los Angeles Central Criminal Court in 1992 rested on the defendant's plea that he was "a cybernetic organism from the future who was programmed to kill anybody who stood between him and his mission to kill John Connor," a ten-year-old child, who he claimed would grow into the "leader of the human resistance to the machines".

Mr Terminator was charged on 347 counts of homicide, accomplished with many unusual methods. In the case of John Connor's step-parents, what appeared in the pathologist's report as "a crazed stabbing" was, claimed Mr Terminator, the result of his liquid-metal structure undergoing metamorphosis into a huge blade. His defence attorney described this as "an unfortunate accident, one that could happen to any cybernetic polymorph".

Prosecuting attorney David Barringstein, cross-examining, described the claim as "fabricated nonsense" and a "clear-cut case of a fictitious insanity plea", at which point a long metal rod reached over from the dock and pinned him to the wall through his brain. As his skull disintegrated, and the shredded remains of his cerebral cortex dribbled in a cascade of blood to the floor, he croaked out the words, "no further questions, Your Honour," and died.

The jury returned a unanimous verdict of "guilty" and Mr Terminator was sentenced to death.

Electronics experts removed his power source and he sat on Death Row, a broken man, until, on the morning of September 14th, he was led to the electric chair. Unfortunately, the 10,000 volt charge revived him, and he swiftly killed all the guards and escaped. His present whereabouts are unknown.

THE CHEESE KILLER

Dr Martin Sparrow became notorious in the 1930's as one of the decade's most bizarre murderers. In the words of the distinguished clinical psychologist Dr Bernard Piltsdown, Sparrow was "mad as a fucking hatter". Researchers could never discover the origin of his psychosis, but he told the police after his arrest that, as a small child, he had been forced by his parents to eat a selection of after-dinner cheeses, when he wanted blancmange.

Quite how this incident turned him into a psychopath, no-one knows. All we can know for certain is that on Monday 13th March, 1934, a woman was discovered strangled in a room at the Royal Seedy Hotel, Bayswater. By her side, on the bed, was a Stilton.

At the time, police thought nothing of it, believing that the killer had panicked and, understandably, had forgotten his cheese in his rush to leave the room. Detectives dusted the Stilton for prints, but when none were found, they ate it.

Two months later they were to regret this, with the discovery of a woman's body in a flat in Earls Court. Again, she had been strangled, and beside her on the bed lay a roulade of French soft cheese with walnuts round the outside. Now their suspicions were powerfully aroused. Detective Inspector Louis Speck at Scotland Yard decided, on a hunch, to check back through their records of unsolved cases. He found, to his horror, that there were three other cases in the previous twelve months in which cheese had been found at the scene of the crime. In one case, it had been a large piece of Parmesan; in another, a wedge of mature Cheddar; and in a third, a man had been found dumped on a railway embankment with a quarter-pound lump of Port Salut in his throat.

Clearly the killings were the work either of a maniac, or possibly of a very strong and demented mouse. All cheese outlets and grocers were carefully watched. A woman was approached in Bayswater by a man "holding something under his macintosh which smelt of cheese," but when police stopped him, they found no dairy produce. Finally, they took a call from a registered patient of a Dr Martin Sparrow, a GP from Enfield who had a line of blue cheeses on the windowsill in his surgery. Police arrested him, and although at first he claimed he was trying to save money by growing his own penicillin, he eventually cracked and admitted that he was the Cheese Killer.

In court he explained that he wanted to kill the cheese, but since it isn't alive, he had to kill something else instead. Nowadays, he would doubtless have been placed in a secure mental hospital and swiftly turned into a made-for-TV film. In 1934, however, he was simply hanged. The coroner refused to grant his last request that he be sliced into narrow strips with a piece of wire.

DELIA BRYANT

The tale of Delia Bryant is a strange one. Delia was born in 1856, only daughter of Mr and Mrs Reginald Bryant of Richmond, Surrey. Her upbringing was typical of the social climate of the mid-Victorian era. Her father's morals were so strict that when in the bath, he hid his penis behind a small curtain attached to a belt round his waist. The family's pet Yorkshire terrier was forced to take her walks wearing a chastity-belt. The legs of the family piano were not only covered, but fitted with full petticoats, and Delia was once soundly beaten for saying the word"ankle".

Bryant with her final victim, Mr. Beardo

Her parents were also rather snobbish, and Delia had no friends at all, as she was not allowed to play with any of her schoolmates, who were all deemed "too common." Since her schoolmates included Lord Exminster, the Viscount Maudsley, the Duke of Gloucester, three foreign princes and two of Queen Victoria's nieces, it is difficult to imagine who she could have played with.

Not surprisingly, Delia withdrew into a world of her own. She wrote stories to help overcome her solitude. But her father, who believed that "all writers and authors are lascivious, Bohemian degenerates," forbade her this activity when he found out, insisting instead that she occupy herself sewing him a pair of chintz ear-muffs, so that he could use the lavatory without hearing any splashes.

It was at this point that Delia, sweet-natured and timid girl that she was, decided to beat her father around the head with a pair of fire-tongs. This she did, and when the police arrived, she spun them an incredible alibi, involving a Balkan spy-ring, a secret formula, a case of mistaken identity and a heroic struggle. The police left satisfied, her father was deemed to have died in a patriotic attempt to save a national secret from foreign thieves. Delia was completely free. It was the beginning of her career as the most brilliant liar of her generation. Her solitary hours spent in her own imagination had left her with the most extraordinary gift for fabricated alibis in the annals of crime.

In 1876, a young man called Nathaniel Trumpett attempted to force Delia, now 20, to snog him at a dance in Clapham. She pushed him down some steps, and he fell and cracked his head. Realising he was dead, Delia told the police that a spectral headless horseman had materialized from the wall and frightened Trumpett so badly that he had fallen. The coroner recorded a verdict of "misadventure" and Delia once again escaped the gallows.

A few months later, she had an argument with her brother, Bertie, who had told her that he did not care for a new pair of shoes she had bought. The next day Bertie died of acute strychnine poisoning. Delia told the police that her brother had been involved in a homosexual scandal involving a prominent royal and a member of the Cabinet, and was just about to reveal details of the affair.

Over the next ten years, Delia was to murder 28 different people, including all her immediate family, three husbands, two employers and a bank manager. She used her extraordinary powers of invention to write three novels for the publishers Boyston and Crackwell – *Lady Maudesley Bumps 'Em Off*, *The Petticoat Poisoner* and *Lady Maudesley Bumps Off A Few More*. She was halfway through a fourth book when, bored with writing, she strangled her publishers, Charles Boyston and Edward Crackwell, claiming their office had been broken into by a crazed werewolf. Her biographer, Ronald Bettiswood, said in 1984 that "the moral of her extraordinary story seems to be that if you are an attractive young woman, and you get a male police officer, you can bullshit them, no problem."

BLOFELD, ERNST STAVRO

The case of Ernst Blofeld has long fascinated criminologists, who have longed to find out why Blofeld always chose the most elaborate methods of death for his victims when, frequently, far more practical methods were at hand.

Although he had a string of residences around the world, Blofeld generally lived a quiet life at 14, Riddlehurst Rise, Dollis Hill. Neighbours remember him as a quiet type, who "kept himself to himself" and spent much of his time stroking his pet cat. None of the other residents of Riddlehurst Rise can have suspected that behind the net curtains of number 14 lurked the evil genius behind SMERSH – Schmiert Spionam – Death to Spies. Psychologists have been unable to trace the origins of Blofeld's obsession, but when police raided 14 Riddlehurst Rise, they were astonished to find a well-stocked piranha-pool in the basement, as well as a monorail, two stolen submarines, a rocket launching-pad and lots of guards in red boilersuits. Confronted by the arresting officers, Blofeld laughed, saying, "I am sure Miss Longlegs would not want you to do anything rash. She seems anxious to avoid the alligators," and, when handcuffed, shouted, "You are too late! In two minutes from now ten major cities will be vaporized!"

Under interrogation by Detective Inspector Cornish at Dollis Hill Police Station, he would only offer the words, "Guards! Kill him!" He is now in a secure mental hospital near Guildford, where he has not spoken for three years except to say, "all the Bond films have been shit since I stopped being in them."

NIELSON, LESLIE

Star of the *Naked Gun* films and the TV series *Police Squad*, Leslie Nielson is an actor who happens to have nearly the same surname as Dennis Nilsen, a convicted serial killer. His inclusion here is really just to point this out, so the British police don't try and arrest him. Their record's been none too hot recently.

DUNMOW, CHARLES

Charles Dunmow was a classmate of pop superstar Tim Cormack at Fieldstone School in the 1970's. Having left the band at seventeen to study for his exams, Dunmow became caught up in a cycle of bitterness and envy which, as his old friend went on to scale the heights of rock fame and fortune, grew to murderous proportions.

THE "SOLIHULL STRANGLER"

A worrying case for criminal psychologists because of the murderer's obsession with his own celebrity. Society does tend to turn murderers into celebrities, giving them large amounts of newspaper and TV coverage, not to mention devoting books and films to their lives. The theory that this celebrity status might "go to the head" of a particular type of murderer seems borne out in the case of the Solihull Strangler who from the start treated himself as if he were some sort of legitimate star-celebrity figure. A year and a half after his first murder he sent, to every national newspaper, an Information Pack and Press Release, which read:

The **SOLIHULL STRANGLER** has been killing for 18 months now and is already a household name. Currently universally regarded as Britain's leading murderer, the Strangler's ambition is to work abroad, possibly in the United States.

Ruthless, clever and brilliant, the Strangler's distinctive style has led to the bafflement of police officers up and down the country. The Daily Mail called him, "a brutal monster, even by the sick standards of today's sick world", while the Times' Crime reporter has described him as "a psychotic... a killer of such ruthlessness that police have not yet found one solid clue as to his identity".

From humble beginnings, he first came to the attention of the public after killing Neil Kennedy in May of last year. This first killing marked him out as a promising young psychotic, and leading exponent of the English style. His murders could be described as post-modernist, combining as they do the traditional methods of stab-and-strangle with a highly contemporary lack of motive and cleanliness of execution. He draws his influences more from America, with its emphasis on emotional detachment, than from the European tradition of the crime passionnel which, though interesting, usually involves capture and imprisonment. However, he resists the gimmickry of firearms, which are producing a generation of untrained, lowbrow killers who are likely to stay in gangland or their own home territory to find their victims.

The Strangler's work so far is as follows:

NEIL KENNEDY A neat strangulation, simple, but effectively done.

EDWARD SMITH A lesser work. A slight struggle led to a stabbing, which, for many purists, spoiled the overall effect.

LUCY MADDOX Considered by some his most brutal work, but this is an oversimplification. A very simple slaying, but appealing at the lowest level.

GRAHAM PINFOLD Wrongly considered by many as the first in a trilogy of jogger-killings, this is a minor work, only of interest for the increasingly accurate use of the knife.

SUSANNE GEE A very fast killing. By this time, the Strangler's technique was approaching maturity. Much-discussed, and the first of

111

the Strangler's works to really make an impact overseas; winner of the Couteau D'Or at the Cannes Crime Festival.

SARAH DYER Described by the News of the World critic as "the work of a homicidal maniac", other reviews were similarly complimentary. The third and currently the last female.

ALAN BRIGHAM For many, an unsatisfactory work. As the Daily Telegraph noted, "some of the stab wounds were post-mortem", indicating an uncharacteristic lack of self-discipline.

GEOFFREY MALDON A largely experimental work, this rather vicious attack took place in the victim's own home, marking a major advance. Several previous victims had died in this way, but this was the first one to admit the Strangler of his own free will.

Police were profoundly worried by this press release, indicating as it did an alarming development in the media-driven tendency to blur the lines between fact and fiction. Fortunately, they then noticed at the bottom of the page the words "available for interview" and a phone number.

As the Strangler began a life sentence in Dartmoor, his agent negotiated an American TV film and a serialization in a major Sunday tabloid, together with a franchise for "Free the Strangler" T-shirts. Profits and royalties will go to help the Strangler put in a bid to buy Dartmoor when it is privatized, and grant himself a pardon.

INDEX

If you have enjoyed this book, and it has inspired you to go and kill someone yourself, then please write to me c/o the publishers to tell me how you get on. I will be using your replies in my next book, *Latent Loonies I Have Unwittingly Encouraged* - C.F.

"The mega-selling megaseller. Soon to be a film. Ooops – a major film. It's always a major film isn't it? Never just 'a film'."

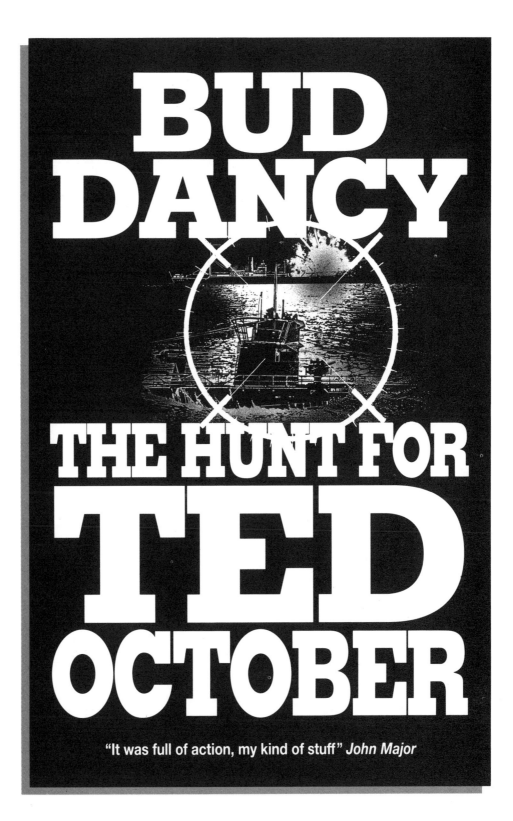

BUD DANCY

THE HUNT FOR TED OCTOBER

"It was full of action, my kind of stuff" *John Major*

Somewhere Above the Arctic Circle

Seabirds wheeled above the slate-gray waters of Bolshoi Sound as the *Blue Volga,* the latest Russian Lenin Class B nuclear submarine, edged its way slowly out toward the icy deeps of the Barents Sea. In the conning tower stood Captain Andrei Vilnius, binoculars clamped to his lined, gray-green eyes, beard flecked with distinguished gray, greatcoat wrapped snugly around his collar to shield him from the bitter cold, and the seagull poo.

Behind him lay the bleak Naval port of Borzhov, and behind that, hundreds of miles of featureless tundra. In front of him lay the open sea. He lowered the binoculars, and his breath steamed in the Arctic air. He looked around him at the wasteland of ice and water, and spoke quietly to himself.

"Did I turn the gas off?" he wondered aloud.

No-one heard this comment; none of the crew was bonkers enough to want to stand in the open air in temperatures of 20 below. But Vilnius had reasons to want to stand there. He wanted to see the Russian mainland disappearing into the mist as the *Blue Volga* made her way out to sea. If things went according to plan, it would be the last time that he ever saw it.

CIA Headquarters, Langley, Virginia

"What do you make of this, Jim?"

Jim Ryman leaned forward toward the Section Chief's desk to examine the sheaf of photographs.

Ryman felt disorientated. Earlier that day he had been in London, where he'd been taking his first vacation in five years. He had wanted to show his young daughter the sights: the Tower, Buckingham Palace, the Raymond Revuebar, the Docklands Light Railway, and the NCP Car Park on the South Bank (Ryman was a car-park fan – "you can tell a lot about a city from its car parks," he would say to his wife, whenever she couldn't sleep). Then the call had come through – emergency. The message on reception at the hotel had simply read, "Your great-aunt is ill. Please call at once." Ryman remembered immediately that "Great Aunt" was the current code for "Middle East", and that "please call" meant "report to Langley". Ryman was on the first plane back to the States.

When he got there he was surprised to learn that, in fact, his great-aunt was in hospital with suspected pneumonia, and that the Middle East was looking much more stable than it had done for some time. However, the Head of Satellite Surveillance had said, "while you're here, drop by. We've got something for you."

The "something" turned out to be a series of reconnaissance photographs. They were originally classified D3, which meant "Rather Dull". The vast majority of satellite photos were D3; some were even D5, "Very Tedious Indeed". However, the Section Head explained that some hotshot at Photo-Interpretation had upgraded these shots to B2, "Actually Quite Interesting".

"I'd say," said Ryman, "that he was being over-optimistic. It's just a Russian sub heading out on an exercise. Can't see why it rates a B2."

"Take a look at the wake," said the Section Head, sipping at his Styrofoam coffee-cup. This was purely a nervous habit, since there wasn't any coffee in it. "Notice anything?"

"Not especially," said Ryman. "The sub's clearing port, probably not doing much over three or four knots. Not much to see."

"It's a single-screw wake on a Lenin-Class boomer," said the Section Head. "Those monsters have been twin-screwed since 1967, and this one's a new design."

"Maybe only one screw's working."

"But she's brand new. Why would they put her to sea with only one screw working?"

"Perhaps it's running-in."

"No new Russian sub would go on a major exercise with only one engine working."

"Is it still under guarantee?"

"On the drawing-board since the late Seventies. Project nearly stalled under Gorbachev, and was believed to have been shelved after the Soviet Union broke up. Obviously the military couldn't bear to see it cancelled after all that work, and they've built it anyway."

"So why all this fuss about the wake?" asked Ryman.

"Because no vessel that size could rely on a single propeller, Jim. Our experts think she must have some other form of propulsion, something new, top-secret, potentially explosive."

"Like – a silent internal turbine drive?" hazarded Ryman.

"Precisely," said the Section Head, grimly. "Take a look at these." He reached into a drawer and drew out a file marked "TOP SECRET. FOR YOUR EYES ONLY".

"Whose eyes?" asked Ryman.

"It doesn't say. It never does. We think maybe it means 'only for your eyes', as in not for any other part of your body."

"But they're photographs," objected Ryman. "Of course they're only for your eyes. You're not going to get a set of photographs marked 'For Your Feet Only'. This seems strange. It's as if whoever writes these classifications doesn't have English as a first language. Could some Middle Eastern agent have penetrated the CIA?"

"Don't be ridiculous," said the Section Head. "Vetting procedures are as tight as they've ever been. You're paranoid, Ryman."

"I guess so," sighed Ryman. "It's just I was talking to Mohammed El-Hezzam over in Electronics the other day, and he was saying something about the final destruction of the Great Satan."

"Forget it, Ryman. You're out of your league. You do your job and let Hussein at Vetting do his. Now, tell me – you're a Naval expert. What do you make of these photos?"

Ryman looked at them.

"They're slightly blurred," he said.

"They were taken by one of our operatives inside the top-secret Russian naval base at Borzhov using a miniaturized camera hidden in one of his shirt-buttons. He risked his life to get these shots."

"All the same, the composition is awful," said Ryman. "Really, the lack of foreground here gives no sense of scale, while on this one, the failed attempt at chiaroscuro lends a frankly amateur feel to the whole thing."

"Look at the side of the submarine, Jim – toward the stern."

"The stern's all I can see. He's missed off the bow completely. All he needed to do was stand a bit further back, or better still, use a different lens. And it's all so blurred. I mean, really – we're the CIA. Can't we afford to give this man a *tripod*, for Chrissakes?"

"Jim, will you shut up?"

"You asked me what I made of these photos."

"I don't mean *aesthetically*, I mean *militarily*."

"Oh, I get it," said Jim. "Well, militarily, they clearly show large oval-shaped ports towards the stern which, taken in tandem with these intake units further forward, clearly indicate that the Russians have perfected the silent internal propulsion drive for which we in the United States have unsuccessfully striven for so long."

"So what are you saying, Jim?"

Ryman leaned forward on the desk.

"What I'm saying," he said, "is that this little baby can move about under water

115

totally undetected by any sonar. This sub could get to within a mile off the coast of the United States and we wouldn't even know it was there."

"Go on."

"Er – well, that's it. Isn't that enough?"

"How does it work?"

"How does it work?" said Jim. "Well, that's kind of difficult to explain. How much do you know about hydro-engineering and pressurized turbines?"

"Diddley-squat, Jim."

"Same here," said Jim. "I think we're in trouble."

The two men looked at each other across the desk.

"Better call Melanie, Jim," said the Section Head. "Tell her she'll be taking Chrissie round Eurodisney on her own."

"Eurodisney's in Paris, sir, not London."

The Section Head looked puzzled. "Sometimes I wonder if our Intelligence is all it should be," he said. "More coffee, Ryman?"

"I haven't had any yet."

"Shoot. Guess I'm kinda worried 'bout this new boomer Ivan's cooked up."

"You seem to have become more stereotypically American in the last ten seconds," observed Ryman, puzzled.

"It's a nervous habit. I always do it under stress," explained the Section Head, and spat in his litter-bin. "Dag-nabbit!" he cried. "Just what in tarnation do these pesky Russkis a-think they're a-doin'?"

Ryman decided to leave him to it; the Section Head was obviously feeling severely stressed. He left the room quietly, leaving his superior muttering something about home runs.

Russian Naval Headquarters, Moscow

Admiral Sergei Tossimov was, at 78, one of the youngest Admirals in the Russian Navy. He was one of the new breed; he had supported Yeltsin against the old Communist hardliners. How well he remembered his family having to queue for three hours under Communism, just to buy a loaf of white bread. Now, under the free market, they only had to queue for two and three-quarter hours, and when they got to the front, there was brown and white bread to choose from.

But Tossimov knew that there were many in the military who bitterly opposed reform. These were men who had lost everything when Communism went: their prestige, their sinecures, and their chance to machine-gun Afghans for a bit of a laugh. But the Red Army, the Navy and Air Force were too huge, too powerful to be got rid of. Within their still-enormous ranks lurked elements who were just waiting for the moment; the moment when they could sweep the Communists back into power. Every point that inflation rose, every rouble that the country went further into debt, these men rubbed their hands with glee. Soon their moment would come, and they, once again would be in power.

This knowledge pissed Tossimov off.

He drank his tea and looked out of his window. The snow was falling gently, and over the road, where for years had stood a poster of Lenin, now stood a poster for Sega Megadrive. They had left the price off the poster; this was because, when quoted in roubles, the price was fourteen yards long.

On Tossimov's desk lay a pile of unopened mail. He sat down again and began to go through it. The first letter was from the BBC in London; it seemed that a show called

116

Jim'll Fix It wanted the Russian Navy to allow an eight-year-old boy to steer an ice-breaker to the North Pole. He threw it away. The truth was that the Russian Navy was so underfunded that the ice-breakers were lacking even the most basic maintenance; in fact, they were under strict orders not to go near any ice. The last one that had hit any had sunk in two minutes.

The next letter was from Captain Andrei Vilnius, Commander of the *Blue Volga*. Tossimov read it, then read it again, said "Oh, shit," several times, and ran out of the office as fast as his 78-year-old legs would carry him.

Aboard the *Blue Volga*

"Status report, Mr Karapov," said Captain Vilnius.

"All systems green. Reactor is normal. Stabilizers are set."

"Excellent." Vilnius looked around him at the bewildering confusion of sonar-screens, lights, switches and buttons that comprised the bridge of a Lenin Class submarine, and remembered the interiors of the submarines he had first commanded back in the late 1940s. Vilnius had been one of the Soviet Navy's youngest ever captains; he was given his first command at the age of twelve, due to administrative error. This type of mistake was common under the unwieldy bureaucracy of Stalin; there was another Andrei Vilnius, a 35-year-old submarine First Lieutenant with ten years' experience, who remained puzzled for the rest of his life as to why an asthmatic child with the same name as him had been promoted over his head.

Vilnius had learned fast. On his first voyage he hadn't even realised that submarines operated below the surface, and had spent the first three hours shrieking "We're sinking! We're sinking!" while the crew simply looked baffled. By the age of 16 he was fully accustomed to being underwater, and spent the next five years learning how not to be sick when they went round corners. At 25 he could read a map and, by 40, he was a reasonable submarine captain.

He had seen huge changes. His first submarine, the *Stalin Is Nice IV,* had been just sixty feet long and the control deck had been childishly simple, which was lucky for Vilnius at the time. The *Stalin is Nice IV* had been diesel-powered and the controls consisted of a lever marked "Up" and "Down" and another marked "Slow" and "Fast". The engines were coin-operated, and they had once been stranded in mid-Atlantic when no-one had the right change. Vilnius smiled when he thought of it; the torpedoes had had a range of three hundred yards and could only hit a stationary target at least fifty yards across. By contrast, the torpedoes on board the *Blue Volga* sought out their targets using computer-controlled sonar guidance systems, and were rumored to be so accurate they could sink a rubber duck at ten miles. In 1983 this rumor was reported back to the CIA, and President Reagan ordered 100,000 rubber ducks to be air-dropped into the North Atlantic.

Those had been the days. The days of the Cold War were but a happy memory for the Russian Navy. In those days they had a role, they knew precisely what they were doing; they were threatening the United States, and the United States was threatening them. It was fun; it provided employment for hundreds of thousands; and it was harmless. In all those years of nuclear paranoia, not one nuclear warhead had even been launched by mistake; not one major population center had been vaporized in a cloud of radioactive dust. But now...

"Dive," said Vilnius, and within seconds came the rumble as the ballast-tanks began to flood and the vast metal bulk of the *Blue Volga* slid beneath the icy waters. When they were at operating depth, Vilnius switched on the ship's intercom system. He was now addressing every crew member.

"Comrades!" he barked, and everyone looked up. The old Communist term "Comrades" was not used any more; indeed, it was forbidden. There was a notice pinned to the ship's noticeboard: "DO NOT CALL EACH OTHER COMRADE. SAY "MATE" OR SOMETHING. SIGNED, B. YELTSIN." Clearly, something was afoot.

"Comrades, now I can reveal to you the nature of our mission. Mother Russia has entrusted us with a magnificent task. We are to test the new Silent Propulsion Drive!"

"Hoorah!" shouted the crew, although none of them knew quite why.

"Switch it on, then," said Vilnius.

The Chief Technical Officer marched proudly over to a control panel marked "TOP-SECRET SILENT PROPULSION DRIVE CONTROL PANEL" (the interior of the *Blue Volga* had been designed by the same person who designed Thunderbird 2).

"Shut down conventional unit," commanded Vilnius, and the reactor was shut off. There was an eerie silence.

"Switch to new top-secret silent propulsion drive."

The Technical Officer pulled the lever marked "On" and, suddenly, there was still an eerie silence.

"Remarkable!" he cried. "The unit is incredible, comrade!"

"That's because it's not on yet," said Vilnius. "Try the lever again."

The Technical Officer threw the lever a second time, and this time there was a low, muffled rumbling, and the *Blue Volga* began to edge forward again.

"It's not really silent, then, strictly speaking," said Second Lieutenant Kirmov.

"Not to us, no," said Vilnius, "but to any other submarine, it is silent, since it cannot be detected on sonar."

"What use is that?"

"It means we can slip past our enemies undetected."

"But we have no enemies."

"I know *that*," said Vilnius, tetchily. "That's because this propulsion system has been in development for years and years. We started developing it way before the Soviet Union fell to bits. We've only just got it to work."

"That's a bit of a shame, comrade."

"Indeed. But it is our duty to test it, and that is what we shall do. Carry on."

The White House Presidential Briefing Room

Jim Ryman was feeling mighty nervous. At just three hours' notice, he had been told that he had to brief the President about the strange goings-on in the Barents Sea.

"Still feeling stressed?" he asked the Section Head of Satellite Surveillance.

"Better believe it, young 'un."

Ryman rolled his eyes and carried on with his preparations. He had a whole series of gels for the overhead projector, and a selection of color transparencies which had to be loaded into the rotary cartridge in the right order.

There was only a half-hour turnaround between briefings. The Economic Advisors had left the room at ten-thirty, and the Security Advisors were supposed to start briefing at eleven. One of the Economic Advisors was still sitting huddled in the corner of the room, moaning "no… no… no" quietly to himself, and would not be shifted. Ryman pressed ahead as quickly as he could, but before he knew it, it was eleven o'clock. The door opened and the President breezed in, with his wife and a trio of aides.

"OK, guys," he said. "What's happening?"

"Mr President," said Ryman, fumbling with the overhead projector. "This briefing concerns the movements of a Russian submarine known to have left Borzhov naval base yesterday morning at 0600 hours."

"Yo!" said the President. "Alright. This is better than Federal Deficits. Lay it on me."

"The name of the submarine is the *Blue Volga*. She belongs to the Lenin Class, type B; a nuclear-powered intercontinental ballistic missile sub."

"Totally bogus!"

"She was spotted leaving port yesterday morning by one of our reconnaissance satellites..."

"Most excellent billion-dollar hardware!" beamed the President.

"We have reason to believe that she is fitted with a revolutionary new drive system which renders her invisible to our sonar."

"Oh, woooow!" intoned the President, turning to his aides. "Hear that, advisory dudes? That makes me feel really safe – NOT!!!!"

His aides signed loudly. The President's PR staff – now the largest single office in Washington – had recently conducted research which suggested that the President was coming across as "out of touch", and that since people were attracted by his youth, he should speak more youthfully. Obviously, like all adult attempts to speak youthfully, he was badly out of date, but the President clearly thought it was doing his image some good; his approval rating had recently gone up from minus 16 to minus 14.

"Naturally, given that the State of Russia is no longer perceived as an enemy, this should theoretically not present us with any worry, although naturally, we would like to discover how the silent drive works…"

"Invisible to sonar is a most excellent way to be for a submariner-dude," said the President. "We should attempt to learn this most interesting propulsion system, most immediatement."

"However…"

"Is there more, Intelligence dude?"

"Indeed, Mr President. We have to consider all possibilities, and..."

"I know, I know!" cried the President, delightedly. "You all think this crazy surfer-captain is one psycho-crazy-apeshit bonkers maniacal dude bent on wholesale destruction and a generally bogus scene."

"...we feel that this is possibly a renegade move by a reactionary pro-Communist element within the Soviet military, yes."

"Woooow!" intoned the President again. "Comforting - NOT!!"

"Please stop saying that," said his wife. "It's two years out of date."

But the President was too caught up to listen.

"Hey, real total *Dr-Strangelove*-scenario weirdness!" he said to Ryman. "Holocaustical bogosity a-gogo. Did you all see *Terminator 2?* Like, wholesale atomic destruction, like real Bay-of-Pigs paranoid scene – oh, woooow. What can we do, CIA dudes? Can we, like, track this submarine down, like is it giving off bad vibes?"

"It's not giving off any vibes at all," said Ryman. "That's why our sonar can't track it."

"Hey, I hate to like come on like a fascist," said the President, "but this guy's got to be stopped, like s-t-o-p-p-e-d, as in vaporized, get hold of the Navy dudes and tell them to like search and destroy."

"As you say, Mr President."

"If this scenario is correct," whispered one of his aides, "then the successful destruction of a hostile nuclear submarine would certainly place your opinion poll rating back up to 80 or even 90 per cent."

As the party left the room, the President's wife whispered to Jim, "This Russian captain better be fish-food by next Friday, or you're back to shovelling shit."

Ryman looked puzzled.

"I've never shovelled shit, ma'am," he said. "I graduated in Modern History from

Harvard, spent five years in Research, then transferred into Intelligence. At no point, in either my academic or military careers, have I shovelled shit."

"It's just a phrase," she said.

"Yo!" came the voice of the President from down the corridor.

Aboard the *Leo Tolstoy*

Two hundred metres below the surface of the North-West Atlantic sat the *Leo Tolstoy*. This was rather worrying – she was an aircraft carrier.

"I think we may be sinking," said Second Lieutenant Oblomov.

"Nonsense," replied Captain Vladimir Sevenyritch. "It is merely a fault in the instrumentation again. This is an old ship." That was certainly true – the *Leo Tolstoy* was the last of the old Soviet Navy's wooden aircraft carriers. Pilots regarded a night-time landing aboard her as a true test of flying skill, chiefly because avoiding the sails was tricky in darkness.

Such was the shortage of funds under Yeltsin that the venerable old *Tolstoy* had been taken out of mothballs at Murmansk and sent out on active duty again. Obviously, with the Cold War ended, her active duties consisted of nothing more than patrolling the waters of the North-West Atlantic and boarding Norwegian trawlers to check that they hadn't been illegally catching whales. On the last occasion they had boarded a trawler whose crew had missed the whale, but harpooned a Greenpeace activist clinging to its dorsal fin. The Greenpeace member had then been weighed, dismembered on deck, and his fatty parts used to make tallow and soap. His cagoule had been sold to the Japanese as a delicacy and his beard used in the manufacture of pan-scourers. Captain Sevenyritch had told the Norwegians firmly that it was his duty, under international law, to report them to the United Nations, but he'd forget the whole thing if they'd give him the dead man's jumper. Decent knitwear was still hard to find in Russia. Yeltsin's so-called reforms didn't seem to have made any difference: all the shops ever had were ghastly jumpers that looked like the sort of thing Mick Robertson would have been ashamed to wear on *Magpie*.

Captain Sevenyritch scanned the horizon and sighed. After a lifetime's service in the Soviet Navy, defending his motherland against the imperialist onslaught of capitalist filth, this was all he had to show for it: an ancient ship and days spent telling Norwegians which sea-mammals they could and couldn't catch. It was a joke, anyway, the Russians telling anyone else that they were being environmentally unsound. Sevenyritch knew for a fact that at least one Russian minesweeper was actually spending its time sweeping lobsters and then selling them in Oslo; while two C-class attack submarines went round a hundred yards apart, with a net strung between them, catching several tons of haddock a day. This was the free-market economy in action. There were even rumors that the destroyer *Czars In Their Eyes* was hunting whales using nuclear missiles. It was catching large numbers of whales, although the meat would not be edible for another 30,000 years.

"Was it all for this?" thought Sevenyritch. Were all the heroic struggles of the Soviet state merely for this – a chance for Russians to start making profits out of their fellow-countrymen?

Suddenly, these thoughts were interrupted by the ship's radio informing Sevenyritch that he was to go to action stations.

"Hoist full sail!" he cried. Clearly, something big and exciting was afoot. The entire Russian Navy was going on full alert. What could possibly be happening?

Aboard the *USS Oprah Winfrey*

"More chicken with asparagus and wild mushroom sauce, sir?"

It was chow time aboard the *Oprah Winfrey,* the newest Class L United States Navy attack submarine. The *Oprah* was actually the GTi version, capable of 0-20 knots in 35 seconds; it had stereo sonar, power-assisted steering and a polarized-glass periscope as standard. The ship's cook, Claude-Pierre Rouvert, was one of the best sauce-makers in the US Navy. He had served in the Gulf campaign, producing a superb chicken in white wine and shallot sauce even under the threat of Iraqi missile attack.

"Thank you, Claude-Pierre."

Captain James Logan dabbed his lips with his napkin. Life aboard a US submarine was certainly easier since the ending of the Cold War. Now that Ivan was busy running up debts and building branches of McDonalds, sub crews could concentrate on learning new skills for a changing world. There were still plenty of goofballs around with access to deadly weapons, plenty of unstable countries led by crazies who might plunge the world back into the dark days of nuclear paranoia. But the Air Force could deal with them. On board a submarine, the chief concern was improving the Quality of Life.

"Colombian or Brazilian espresso, sir?"

"Are we out of Kenyan?" said Logan.

"With respect, sir, Kenyan is somewhat too mild to make good espresso. It is better as a breakfast coffee, where its light, pleasant aroma is ideal with fresh bread and croissants."

"Very well, Colombian then, please."

The *Oprah* had been two months at sea, cruising the North Atlantic, her sonar sounding out all foreign submarines, hoping to find one who could give Lieutenant Cluskey the last answer he needed to complete the *New York Times* bumper crossword. Crewman Taylor was on the last chapter of the novel he was writing, while the Chief Engineer, "Studs" Bronsky, was busy practising his flute.

"That's nice, Studs."

"It's Mozart. Personally, I feel I'm still a little too staccato in the Adagio."

There was no question about it, life aboard a nuclear attack submarine had certainly changed since the old days. Everyone still went through the motions: they listened for other submarines, they primed and checked their torpedoes, they took part in exercises. But then Fleet Command had sent them this message:

CODE – 235   FLEET COMMAND TO OPRAH WINFREY STOP PROCEED 13 DEG W. 47 DEG N. AWAIT FURTHER INSTRUCTIONS STOP

The Captain had swiftly wired back:

CODE – 446   OPRAH WINFREY TO FLEET COMMAND STOP THANK GOD FOR THAT STOP ZILCH TO DO STOP WHAT'S THE SCAM? STOP

The return signal from Fleet Command had also been swift:

CODE – 978 FLEET COMMAND TO OPRAH WINFREY STOP DON'T BE NOSEY STOP IT'S SECRET ISN'T IT? STOP

Intrigued, Captain Logan had despatched another signal:

CODE – 453 OPRAH WINFREY TO FLEET COMMAND STOP DON'T BE A

TEASE STOP WHAT'S UP? GO ON OH PLEASE TELL I WON'T TELL ANYONE
ELSE STOP

Fleet Command had responded immediately:

CODE – 433 FLEET COMMAND TO OPRAH WINFREY STOP NOT SAYING
ANYTHING ELSE STOP JUST PROCEED TO SPECIFIED CO-ORDINATES
STOP

Logan's reply had been coded and transmitted within minutes:

CODE – 211 OPRAH WINFREY TO FLEET COMMAND STOP YOU ARE
HORRID AND I HATE YOU STOP TELL ME OR ELSE STOP

The reply had been beamed via the military satellite network down into the Atlantic:

CODE – 132 FLEET COMMAND TO OPRAH WINFREY STOP FOR FUCK'S
SAKE STOP STOP FARTING ABOUT YOU BIG GIRL'S BLOUSE STOP
PROCEED NNW AT ONCE STOP AND NO RETURNS STOP

"Damn!" cried Logan as the message clattered off the teleprinter. "Fleet Command
have sent 'and no returns'!"

"You ain't gonna let 'em get away with that, are ya?" enquired "Tex" Stetson.

"I certainly am not," replied Logan. "We'll show 'em nobody fools with the *USS
Oprah*. Send a message!"

A few minutes later, Fleet Command's radio operative was bemused to see the
following communique chattering off his machine:

CODE – 978 OPRAH WINFREY TO FLEET HEADQUARTERS STOP YOU
SMELL STOP YES YOU DO YOU SMELL OF POO STOP THRICE OVER AND
NO RETURNS STOP

The reply followed a few minutes later:

CODE – 344 FLEET COMMAND TO OPRAH WINFREY STOP IF YOU GO
YOU'LL GET SWEETIES STOP

Shortly afterwards, the *USS Oprah Winfrey* altered course and began to track north-
west across the Atlantic. Clearly, something was afoot.

10 Downing Street, London

British Prime Minister John Major was just spreading some Happy Shopper margarine
on his toast when the phone rang.

"Norma!" he shouted. "Finish my dippy-soldiers, will you? My eggy's nearly ready."

Leaving his toast half-sliced, he picked up the receiver. It was his Press Secretary.

"Ready for the briefing, sir?"

"Oh, God." He didn't want to have to face the day's press. Invariably, the national
newspapers said horrible things about him. All he really wanted was to eat his boiled
egg, and then flip the TV on and watch England get trounced at cricket. At the moment,

they were mid-way through the third match of their Test series against the Faeroe Islands. The Faeroe Islands had won the first two games, the first by 567 runs, the second by a mere 543. But for the third Test, the selectors had put some fresh blood into the team. Lord Hailsham was in as a pace-bowler, while Phillip Schofield was batting number three. It promised to be an exciting game. The key thing would be to dispose of the Faeroe Islands' danger-man, Lars Svenesson, a herring-packer from Smorginsvoot. Although asthmatic, and one-armed following a horrific herring-packing accident, he had knocked the England bowlers for 213 in the second Test, before giving up his innings voluntarily and going in to watch the telly.

"Do I have to come and look at the papers?" asked Major, plaintively. "The cricket starts in twenty minutes."

"Yes, you do," said the Press Secretary. He felt sorry for the Prime Minister; he'd been under such pressure for the previous year or so that he was beginning to shy away from going to the Commons, and liked to withdraw into his shell, like a child that's unhappy at school. Only a week earlier he had missed a vital Commons debate on European unemployment initiatives on the grounds that he "had a verruca".

"But I wunt to watch the cricket, oh yes, that is what I wunt," said Major. "This is a vital game. If we can't beat the Faeroe Islands we're going to have real trouble next summer when we play Antarctica."

"I'm sorry, sir," said the Press Secretary firmly, "but you've got to come and see the papers. You have to keep in touch."

"Oh, all right. But I wunt to eat my eggy first."

Fifteen minutes later, Major was seated in his office while his Press Secretary briefly summarised the main stories and editorial lines being taken by the national press for him. It wasn't, overall, a bad day: one of the tabloids' front pages read MAJOR IS RUBBISH AND MUST GO, and another read PLEASE STOP BEING PRIME MINISTER NOW. Two of the qualities led on opinion polls suggesting that 98% of the population thought he was a "shit" Prime Minister, with only 2% saying he was "only a bit shit". All in all, he'd got off quite lightly.

"Can I go and watch the cricket now?"

"No. You've got to go to the Commons. You've got to make a statement about the economy."

"Oh, God," said Major. Suddenly, the phone buzzed again. Major picked it up.

"Green eggs and ham," said a voice, and rang off.

"Oh, whoopee!" said Major. At last – something exciting! "Green eggs and ham" was a secret code.

"Who was that?" asked the Press Secretary.

"Can't tell you. Even if I wunted to. You're not important enough," smirked Major. "Only I am. Because I'm Prime Minister. I am. No-one believes me, but I am."

Major trotted out of the room and into a smaller office down the passage where he picked up a phone and pressed the button marked TOP SECRET SCRAMBLER HOT LINE (again, designed by the same man who did Thunderbirds).

"Hello?"

"Yo, John, most excellent Prime Minister! Señor Clintono here, your main man, Number One dude!"

"Hello, Bill," said John. "Are you still as unpopular as me, oh yes, as unpopular?"

"Unpopularity still uno grosso problemo, but hey! What can you do, John, my friend? They vote you in because they say they want change. Then, the moment you change anything, they want you out again. Crazy! Anyhows, my man, this is not the point of this most secretivious transatlanticated telecommunication, dude. Guess what?"

"I don't know. Something's happened?"

"Guess!"

"No, go on, tell me, oh yes, tell me."

"No – guess, dude! You'll never guess!"

"Tell me, oh yes. That is what I wunt."

"Get this, man. The Russians have lost a submarine."

Major was baffled by this. "Lost a submarine, Bill?"

"Like, vanished, man. Gone. Left harbour and sunk without trace."

"Submarines are supposed to do that, oh yes, supposed to."

"But it's gone, man. Real gone sub. But like, Cold War's over, man, he can't be trying to defect. So what is he like doing?"

"I do not know. I am not sure that I wunt to know."

"I'll tell you what he's doing, man. He's gone apeshit, man. Like, a lot of these military dudes are kinda, you know, they kinda want the Cold War back. We've got a lot of those types here too. Half the Army generals want the Cold War back, like in all its bogus-ness, man, 'cos then we give 'em more money and they have something to do."

"So what are you saying, Bill?"

"I'm saying, man, that this submarine has got like thirty multiple-headed nuclear warheads on board, and a freak at the wheel. He might just decide to like waste a few cities, just to get us all hyped up a bit. Totally bogus."

"Can't we find it?" said Major. "Use sonar, or something?"

"That's the major bummer, man. We can't. This submarine's got some like new engine or something that's undetectable. We can't find it. We don't know where it is."

"Oh dear, oh dear," said Major. "That is, indeed, not good news. Not good news at all."

"We're on the case. The whole Navy's out looking for this wacko, and so is Ivan, man. But, hey, you know, it's like, there's a lot of sea out there."

"Indeed, yes. Well, I will see what I can do," said Major. "Goodbye, Bill. Love to Hillary."

"Thanks, man. Hi to the Norma babe too. Ciao!"

Major put the phone down and thought for a second.

"Norma!" he shouted. "I think my problems might be solved."

Aboard the *USS Kermit the Frog*

400 miles east of Newfoundland, where the Grand Banks fall away into the deep abyss of the Atlantic basin, the *USS Kermit the Frog,* the latest "Muppet" class destroyer, was tracking steadily north-east. A hundred miles due south the *USS Great Gonzo* was tracking a parallel course.

Captain Edward Fairisle scanned the horizon, which was a completely pointless activity, since they were looking for a submarine. So instead he went to the bridge, and radioed the *USS Dr Teeth.*

"*Kermit* to *Teeth.* Any luck?"

"No."

"Keep scanning."

"Of course I'll keep scanning. What did you think I was going to do – turn all the lights out and go to bed?"

"No need to be like that."

"Tell me my job. Mind your own ship, butt-head. OK?"

"And the same to you, asshole!"

Fairisle switched the radio off and reflected sadly that Navy discipline was not what it was before the Cold War ended. The lack of a real enemy had led to sloppiness. Once sailors had called the captain "sir". Now most of them called him "Ed", or even worse, "My man".

To make matters even worse, the CIA were flying some wet-behind-the-ears rookie out to tell him his job. This Jack Ryman, whoever in hell he was, was on his way in a "Rattletrap" class R-4 transport helicopter. Well, Fairisle would make him suffer. The Navy weren't no picnic. No Langley hotshot could calmly march out from behind his desk and tell him how to look for a submarine. No sir.

A distant buzzing on the cold, gray horizon announced the approach of the chopper.

Aboard the Rattletrap, Jack Ryman was miserable. The weather over the West Atlantic was windy and squalling, and there were no sickbags aboard a military chopper. All there was was a large notice sellotaped to the inside of the door: A SICK MARINE IS A NO-GOOD USELESS-PIECE-OF-SHIT MARINE. As if this wasn't enough, another notice read: REAL MEN DON'T PUKE, and a third said: VOMIT HOME TO MOMMY. Ryman had voided the entire contents of his stomach hours before, and they sat around him in a malodorous puddle. Periodically, he could hear the pilot on the radio: "The no-good useless-piece-of-shit mommy's boy from the CIA has puked, sir, in a way that no proper soldier would. Permission to take him home and tuck him up with his My Little Pony, sir."

Ryman had the distinct impression that the military did not take kindly to CIA people encroaching on their patch. But he had been sent by the President himself to take charge of the operation. He had a hunch, and if his hunch was correct, he needed to be there in person. If he read the situation right, this man Vilnius who had stolen the submarine was a subtle, intelligent man. And he had a sneaking suspicion he knew what was going on in Vilnius' head...

"We're here, boy," said the voice of the pilot.

"What do you mean? We're still hundreds of feet in the air."

"Yo' gettin' out here."

"Can't you land on the ship?"

"No can do. Orders, Mr Ryman. Not enough fuel, conditions too hazardous. And basically, we want to see you dangle on a rope, jackass."

So Ryman was lowered on a rope down to the deck of the ship. Freezing, teeth chattering and soaking wet, he was led to the Captain's cabin.

"Jack Ryman?" said Fairisle.

"Yes, sir."

"Pleased to have you on board this uncomfortable combat destroyer. I expect you'll be wondering where the guest rooms are?"

"A bunk will be fine, sir."

"This ain't no pleasure cruise, Ryman."

"Obviously, sir, no."

"Ain't no fuckin' deck-quoits in the Navy, you long yellow streak of piss. We're real men, Ryman. We don't work behind no desk and we don't have no fancy ways. You try anything and I'll bust your ass."

"Do I get the impression you don't really want me here?"

"I bin in the Navy thirty years, Ryman. The sea is my wife, my mistress, my family and my next-door neighbor. You don't know shit. Why they sent you here I don't know, but one thing I sure as hell do know – you don't have no authority here."

"All I desire, sir, is that a particular procedure be followed in capturing the missing Russian submarine. You see, I have studied the psychological profiles of the Captain, Andrei Vilnius, together with his service history and family background..."

"Oh, well have you now?" said Fairisle. "Well, let me tell you this, CIA-boy. You can take your psychological profile and you can shove it up a cow's ass."

"That's a very interesting image you've chosen."

125

"Image, horseshit."

"Cows, horses. Did you grow up on a farm, by any chance? Any childhood incidents you associate with animals?"

"You people don't know nothing," said Fairisle contemptuously. "If this was up to you, this Russky'd be launching a nuclear attack on New York and all you'd want to do would be to discuss the phallic symbolism of missiles."

"It could provide useful insight, yes."

"Listen, Jello-brain. This crazy mother's stole a submarine, he's headed for the United States, and when we find him, we're gonna blow him out the water. What'choo say to that, smart-ass?"

"I'd say you have an attitude problem, Mr Fairisle."

"Oh do you? Well, my attitude is this – I don't like you. Go and peel four tons of potatoes for ship's supper."

"What's on the menu?"

"Four tons of boiled potatoes."

"Terrific."

Aboard the *Blue Volga*

While the entire Russian and United States navies were sweeping every quadrant of the Western Atlantic in their frantic search for the missing nuclear sub, Captain Vilnius was guiding the *Blue Volga* gently into the mouth of the Thames. It was a tricky maneuver: the sand-banks meant the water became very shallow in places. Vilnius guided the huge Lenin-Class vessel through the awkward deep-draught channels.

"Raise periscope," he said. When he peered through, he could see Southend to the north. Switching to high magnification, he could see that Jim Davidson was due to play the Marine Theater. He made a mental note, if his scheme worked, to get tickets.

"Captain," came the voice of Second Lieutenant Pidgin. "May I ask a question?"

"You may."

"What on earth are we doing here?"

"We're lost."

Pidgin looked disbelieving. The *Blue Volga* carried the very latest, state-of-the-art navigation technology: variable-frequency hi-wibble sonar, auto-guided rudder-systems, magneto-field trim-orientation guidance computers, and a big map marked "Underwater" as well as a thick book called *A-Z Ocean Floor*. It was unthinkable that a Captain of Vilnius' experience could have thought he was on the Eastern seaboard of the Americas when, in fact, he was off Southend. Pidgin smelt a rat. This was partly due to the stowaway rat that had died under the main control console.

"Captain," said Pidgin. "Is it possible that all our navigation systems have had simultaneous malfunction?"

"It is unlikely, I admit," agreed Vilnius. "And yet, almost incredibly, that seems to be what has actually occurred – oh my God! Look!"

Red lights were flashing all over the ship, reading RADIATION ALERT, VERY VERY DANGEROUS (the Thunderbirds designer at it again).

The crew of a nuclear submarine are highly trained for such emergencies. Their psychological-stress course ensures a clear-headed response, while their military drill ensures that all safety procedures are carried out, calmly and quickly, in order to minimize the danger. They had faced a reactor leak many times in simulated situations.

"Help! help! We're all going to die!" they cried. Obviously, no amount of training in simulated situations can ever quite live up to the real thing. Bridge Officer Sputin, for

126

example, who had been commended at the Nivgi-Novisibusk Naval Training College for his command potential, was supposed to be directing the engineering personnel to check all coolant-duct seals; he was crouched under a chair shouting "switch everything off!" very loudly. According to the Submarine Services Training Procedures, Third Lieutenant Kransky was supposed to send a top-secret coded signal to all nearby Russian vessels; instead, he had fainted.

"For heaven's sake," yelled Vilnius. "Call yourselves seamen?"

"We're all going to die!" they cried.

"In a horrible way," added someone else, helpfully.

"Silence!" cried Vilnius. "Keep a hold of yourselves, you fools. It seems we have a reactor emergency. We do not know how serious it is..."

"Anything involving raw uranium is serious in my book," shouted a crewman.

"Hear, hear."

"As you know, comrades, the reactor for this vessel was designed by the finest scientific brains in the Soviet Union..."

If this was meant to reassure people, it didn't. In fact, now they were utterly hysterical. The finest scientific brains might have designed it, but the finest bureaucratic brains had costed it. Deciding it was too expensive, they had removed all the tiresome safety devices, reasoning that if anything went wrong with it, it would be nowhere near them when it happened, so it didn't really matter. (This problem, of course, was by no means exclusive to the Soviet Union.)

"Very well," said Vilnius. "I shall consult the manual."

From a small cupboard on the bridge he selected a green-covered volume entitled *The Lenin-Class B Nuclear Submarine – An Owner's Manual*. Flipping to the section headed "Reactor", he read aloud: "Your Lenin-Class B is fitted with the superior D-239-S nuclear reactor, providing smooth acceleration and economical running for years to come. The D-239-S runs on uranium fuel rods, which should be fitted ONLY by an authorized Russian Federation Navy dealer. It is not recommended... blah, blah, blah... nothing much use here..."

"Hurry, captain!"

"Hang on, I'll try the bit at the back – ah, here we are – "Troubleshooting". He studied the page:

TROUBLESHOOTING Some Common Problems and their Solutions

PROBLEM	CAUSE	SOLUTION
Submarine will not start	No fuel-rods	Fit fuel-rods
Submarine will not sink	Insufficient ballast	Check ballast + tanks
Submarine sinks, but will not rise again	Ballast-tank pumps faulty	Check and replace
No idea where you are	Sonar malfunction	Surface and have a look
Crew are bored	Long voyage	Travel Chess
Torpedo will not fire	Dead shark in tube	Remove shark
You are under attack	War has broken out	Negotiate peace settlement
Crew suddenly die	Radiation leak	Get the fuck out

"Ah," said Vilnius. "Er – well, there isn't anything for our current situation. However, I am a reasonable man. I can see some of you are very worried..." (Sputin had just chewed off one of the periscope-handles) "... so I will allow any of you who wish to leave, to do so."

Five minutes later, the *Blue Volga* was empty apart from Vilnius.

"I knew they'd fall for it," he said, switching off the Radiation Alert signs. "Never fails."

The Ministry of Defence, London

"So you see my problem, gentlemen, oh yes, my problem."

The Navy Chiefs of Staff looked at each other.

"Er – we sort of do, Prime Minister."

"It's just, basically, that I am up the excremental estuary with no means of propulsion, and I wunt something to boost my popularity. That is what I wunt."

"We see that, but..."

"You see, Maggie, my predecessor, was as unpopular as me until the Falklands, jammy cow, oh yes, jammy cow. What I would really like, gentlemen, is if you could locate this rogue submarine, and then destroy it with a nice big bang and make sure the TV cameras are there first."

"But you won't see anything. It's underwater."

"They can get cameras underwater, can't they? What about Jacques Cousteau? He had cameras underwater, so he could film jellyfish and coral and things, yes, jellyfish and coral. I wunt the same thing, only to film a submarine exploding, oh yes, exploding. That is what I wunt. And I wunt it on the nine o'clock news. Anyone know the cricket score, by the way?"

"The Faeroe Islands were 897-1 at lunch."

"That's what happens when you bowl under-arm."

"There are only two problems, Prime Minister. Firstly, we don't know where this submarine is, and secondly, the Americans are looking for it too, and if they find it, their ships are under orders to destroy it."

"Of *course* they are. That's because Clinton's as unpopular as me. The point is, if we can blow up a submarine that's threatening to destroy London, I'll be popular again."

"But it isn't threatening to destroy London."

"The public don't know that, do they? As far as they're concerned, it's a submarine with a madman on board, full of big atomic bombs that can destroy the whole of South-East England. Come to think of it, maybe that would be a better idea – the rest of the country would love it."

Deptford, London

Ted October crossed the main road and made his way, through the rows of 1960s flats, towards the south bank of the River Thames as it rounded the long, majestic sweep of Greenwich Reach. In his hand he clutched last week's issue of *Exchange and Mart,* and in the nondescript-looking bag by his side was £6500 in cash. He felt nervous: this was not really an area of London in which walking round with that sort of money was wise. Actually, there is no part of London where walking around with that sort of money is wise. Walking around with that sort of money isn't wise, full stop.

But there was such a bargain in the offing that Ted just couldn't resist it. He hadn't believed his eyes when he saw it. He'd been looking for a Vauxhall Cavalier – the fuel-injected version. He'd been through the whole of the "Cars" section, circling likely purchases with his biro. Then, just for a laugh, he'd had a quick flip through "Boats for Sale". It always puzzled him; who was going to buy a boat through *Exchange and Mart*? OK, maybe a little dinghy or an inflatable. But anyone seriously contemplating shelling out tens of thousands of pounds on any sort of navigable watercraft would surely go to some specialist publication? Or maybe that was the point – the chance element? Perhaps the sort of person who bought *Exchange and Mart* to see whether there were any pedigree Cairn Terrier puppies for sale might turn the page and, on impulse, decide to buy a yacht instead?

Anyway, whatever the truth, he'd seen the ad almost by accident. Tucked at the bottom of the page, beneath an ad for an eighteen-foot cabin-cruiser:

FOR SALE, Submarine; nclr. pwr, ballst. missls. inc. V.G.C., one owner. Offers Moscow 322-759.

He'd blinked several times, and assumed it was a joke. So, apparently, had everyone else, for when, after one too many pints of lager that night, he'd decided to phone the number for a joke, he'd got through to a distinguished, military-sounding Russian whose English seemed very good. Yes, he'd said, the submarine was for sale. It was all above board: the Russian Navy was keen to get rid of some of its over-large fleet.

Ted offered six thousand pounds. The Russian argued him up to six and a half, and said he'd deliver.

Now Ted stood by the Thames, glancing at his watch. He had a strange feeling that he was going to be made a royal fool of, that was why he hadn't told any of his friends, not even his wife, about his bargain.

"I've been stitched up like a kipper," he muttered to himself. "I bet this is a wind-up."

As he spoke, a huge nuclear ballistic-missile submarine surfaced and the hatch opened.

"Hello," shouted the captain. "Are you Ted?"

"Er – yes," said Ted.

"Here it is, then."

Vilnius got out the inflatable and rowed ashore. A group of small boys gathered in a knot by the quayside and were discussing the submarine amongst themselves.

"Those are crap, those are."

"They're not."

"They are. They're crap. My Dad had one."

"Your Dad never had one."

"He bloody did. He bloody did and you're a liar. They're crap. He's got a better one."

"What one?"

"He's a got a bigger one."

"Where does he keep it?"

"In the sea."

Vilnius and Ted shook hands.

"She's all yours," said Vilnius. "All the documents are in a drawer on the bridge."

"Er – I think I'd like a test drive first."

"Certainly. Get aboard."

As the *Blue Volga* sank beneath the Thames again, leaving fifty extremely puzzled Japanese tourists furiously waving their Camcorders from the deck of a river-cruiser, Ted asked Vilnius, why?

"There are many reasons," said Vilnius. "This ship was designed for one use, and one use only."

"A nuclear first-strike," said Ted.

"As you say. At the time this ship was blueprinted, there were those in the Kremlin who believed that if a silent submarine could be built, we would be able to wipe out the US once and for all..."

"Seems a bit odd now."

"Well, exactly. I mean, that's all it does. It goes underwater and drives about a lot. That's no use to anyone, is it?"

"So why sell it?"

"Market economy. It's what we're all being encouraged to do, isn't it? It's a free market. We must exploit our assets. Since we don't have any use for this any more, I thought I might as well sell it. It's fully MOT'd."

10, Downing Street, London

"Phone call, John."

"Who is it?"

"Clinton again."

Major took the receiver.

"Any luck, Bill?"

"Negative, my most excellent friend. All our AWACS, SOSUS systems and surface fleet have failed to find the *Blue Volga*. However, we do have a satellite picture showing a heat-bloom in the Thames just north of Deptford."

"Oh. That'll be the huge radioactive discharge from Aldermaston I'm not allowed to tell anyone about."

"Oh. Well, looks like we're still in the deepo shitto, my man."

"Yes, indeed."

"You know, my man, I think you and I suffer from being the first post-Cold-War leaders. We have no-one to blame, man. No bogeyman!"

"I know what you mean."

"Shit, man. Tell you what. If the Russians won't blow up New York any more, why don't you do it?"

"Eh?"

"Totally bongo idea! You've got this Trident shit, man, cost a whole bunch of bread and it's no use whatsoever. Why don't you launch a nuclear strike against us, and I'll blow you up, and then I'll be popular again, and you can pretend it wasn't us, but Saddam Hussein. Then you can nuke him, and you'll be popular too!"

Major thought for a second. "It all seems to have gone from being farfetched to being utterly farfetched," he mused. "Hang on." He rang off and reached for his address book. It was time to hand over to Jeffrey Archer.

BUSINESS

"The bestselling business title, now in paperback."*

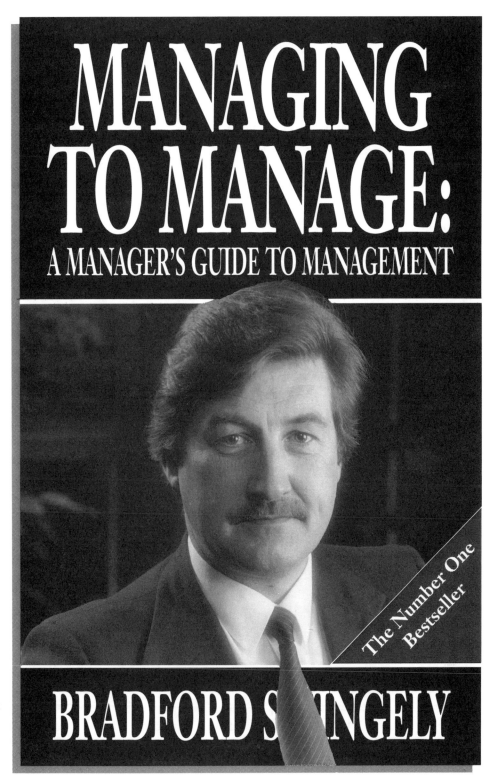

MANAGING TO MANAGE:
A MANAGER'S GUIDE TO MANAGEMENT

The Number One Bestseller

BRADFORD S INGELY

*(At a saving of 48.2% on the hardback price, tax-deductible over 3 years for Schedule D payers.)

Acknowledgements

This book has been many years in development. If it has a date of conception it was one evening in November 1989. As fate would have it, I had just dined at White's with my fellow captain of industry, Sir Ivan Gobbscheidt. We had retired to the members' lounge when he mentioned to me that he had in mind the notion of writing "a Bible for British management", based on his many years at the industrial and corporate coalface. British industry, he suggested, had lost its way, had forgotten the basic ingredients of manufacturing and commercial success, and had rested for too long upon its laurels as the founding father of the first, coal-led industrial revolution. He told me, over cigars and an excellent '79 Port, that he hoped his book would in some way halt this decline, or at the very least cause us to question the structure upon which our commercial nationhood is based, thereby preventing the same, all-too-basic, mistakes being made again by future generations.

Listening to him, I could not help but be struck by the nobility of such a project. It surely is the duty of every successful businessman to do exactly as Sir Ivan suggested: to pass on what little knowledge he has culled through his involvement in business, to attempt to cross-fertilise ideas and experience with other areas of commercial enterprise, to try and break down the barriers and the formality that have for too long stifled the growth of British industry. It was therefore at that moment that I decided I, too, would write such a book. More importantly, I would get mine to the market before Sir Ivan had even approached a publisher. In short, I resolved to stitch Sir Ivan up like a kipper, and to teach him a business lesson that he was never likely to forget: "Never believe that anyone is your friend."

I have neither the time or space to thank all those involved in the writing of this book. There is also the danger that if they are mentioned, that they will want a slice of the almost obscenely large profits from its publication. I will, however, thank those who represent no threat.

Firstly, I would like to thank my father, who is dead. It would also be churlish to neglect the sterling efforts of Professor Gorem Miklaub of London University, who read an early draft of the book, passing constructive criticism upon it, until it slowly dawned on him that it was remarkably similar to an essay of his published in 1954 whilst he was junior professor at the University of Leeds. Sadly, his ability to do anything other than become bitter and twisted has been much reduced by the financially ruinous court action he took out against me last year, before he realised the financial might I have at my disposal, the sheer unadulterated nastiness of my lawyers, and the fact that he was not entitled to legal aid.

Finally, I must address those involved in the compilation of the case studies that make up this book. I should especially like to thank all those who assumed that their contributions, exposing the failings of the companies they work for, would remain anonymous. Instead, I shall reward them with a large font and bold typeface. **ALAN DAVIES** of the Torq Corporation (who told me all about the problems in the cost-control unit, and the investigation of company assets by the Fraud Squad). **MELANIE JALFREY** of McNaughton (that's not the Melanie who works at the

Glasgow plant. It's the other one, with the blond hair. Quite tall, about 5'9") who told me how much she hated all the senior management and how "piss-poor" they were at their jobs. And, finally, **ROGER MELSON** of Dayter Inc, who informed me about problems in the construction and delivery of the new MOD Radar Defence system. Indeed, to Roger I also owe an apology: I let slip that it was you who had passed this information on to me, so it was probably my fault that your really rather worthless life ended so abruptly last year in an as-yet-unexplained gas explosion.

BRADFORD SWINGELY
LARGEHOUSEIN
BERKSHIRE

SEPTEMBER 1993

Contents

CASE-STUDY ONE:

COLUMBINE SOFTWARE

I was invited to consult on Columbine Software in the summer of 1989 by their then-chairman, Marvin P. Halsteed. The company had grown up during the boom years of the 1980s, at a time when the computer market, and in particular that of personal computers and office-based computer software, had mushroomed into a multi-million-pound business. Although not on the scale of an IBM or Compaq, Columbine had nonetheless cornered a small but significant section of the British market, through their patenting of an ingenious software package.

The success of the program lay in its near universal application. It was not restricted to any particular work environment, or business, but was equally popular amongst accountants, order clerks, nurses, engineers – anybody who used a VDU in the course of their work. The "Playsafe"™ programme was simple in its conception.

For some while software manufacturers had been growing rich on the sales of business programs such as Applewrite, WordPerfect, Microsoft Word, and so on. Yet market research consistently demonstrated that, in fact, what most people were looking for at work was an excuse *not* to have to use these work programs. At that time, most employees were having to wait until after work before being able to use their office computers for games.

This was where Columbine scored, devising a program that enabled the user to play any computer game on his or her screen (be it Sonic the Hedgehog, Super Mario, Streets of Rage, or tamer examples such as battleships or solitaire), with no risk of discovery by superiors. Or, in the case of the bosses themselves, by those junior to them. The technology was simple: the user would wear an unobtrusive ID, disguised as a button, brooch or tie-clip. A unique sensor, in the front of the terminal, would recognise the user, but at the approach of anyone likely to be upset about the use of the computer for recreational purposes, would immediately cause the screen to show some legitimate data: long rows of figures, sales data, chemical formulae, design drawings or simply text. This made discovery almost impossible.

Backed by a high-profile advertising campaign with two alternative copylines: "Playsafe™. For people who don't really want to work very hard actually" in the broadsheet papers, and "Playsafe™. For lazy bastards" in the tabloids, the system had swept across the nation. Brilliantly, Columbine had homed in on the essential British characteristic of laziness and turned it to their advantage (and enormous profit).

It was here, though, that Columbine's problems began. As their coffers swelled, the entire industrial and corporate edifice of the nation came crumbling down around them. Freed of the requirement to be grown-up, people had lost both the will and motivation to work. In the first year after the launch of the "Playsafe"™ system, the profits of Britain's industrial giants fell to pre-war levels as the productive output of their workforces fell away to zero.

At Conch Petroleum the interdepartmental James Pond tournament meant that the exploration team (a department of 3000 people across five continents) uncovered not one teaspoonful of new oil in an entire twelve-month period. At investment bank Kilm Kenwright McDonald, traders totally failed to notice dramatic market movements on their screens, sold millions of pounds worth of bonds at below their true market value, and plunged the company into receivership. At Gatwick Airport, air-traffic controllers had their worst year on record, recording 46 near misses and 14 fatal air crashes in the skies over Sussex. The tragic loss of over 2,950 lives was, however, soon forgotten when chief controller Malcolm Gainsborough became national champion at Sega Megadrive Football.

The economy was plunged into crisis. Share prices fell to levels lower even than those reached on Black Wednesday. Billions of pounds were pulled from London by international investors who saw Frankfurt, Hong Kong, Tokyo and New York as more attractive and stable alternatives. And as the share prices fell, great British companies became easy prey for foreign takeover bids. Unilever was bought by the Swiss Nestlé Corporation, Barclays Bank fell to Deutsche Bank, and the entire Tesco food chain was bought by a small independently owned kebab shop in Dublin, with a loan secured against the proprietor's Austin Allegro. The Treasury's chief economists, custodians of the national purse, looked hard at their screens in an attempt to comprehend the crisis, but it was too late. Even in that unimaginably boring government department, all the screens were showing was a small blue hedgehog with an unfeasibly small number of spines, desperately collecting gold hoops.

For Columbine Software, the situation was extremely serious. The market was now saturated with "Playsafe"™ and yet their potential customers for any new product, namely the major corporations, had no money to spend. Indeed, thanks to Columbine's product, they were in the business of survival rather than expansion. Cost-cutting was the order of the day: J.P. Morgan, the merchant bank, had recently vacated its plush Thames-side offices for a complex of recently vacated Portakabins on the edge of an abandoned construction site in Droylsden. Marks and Spencer, no longer able to sustain the cost of its stores, had opted for just one outlet – a fruit and vegetable stall at Petticoat Lane market. This would be manned in turn by the chairman and the chief executive, the only two people still employed by the retailing phenomenon of the 1980s (causing immense problems when regular customers attempted to put a pound of tangerines on their charge-card).

To further compound the situation, Columbine itself had fallen foul of the "Playsafe"™ problem. They had no idea of their own financial position. Their accounts department had not operated efficiently for over two years, although they were all very good at Revenge of Shinobi. They had no record of their own stock position, as this too was computer-driven. Worse still, their Research department, the core of any hi-tech company, and upon which Halsteed was relying to provide the next great leap forward in company profits and fortunes, appeared to be operating normally whenever he went to visit them, but had in fact, since the launch of "Playsafe"™ itself, thought of nothing new whatsoever, apart from how to get past the Gatekeeper of Doom into Level 7 of Dragonmaster's Labyrinth. Under the influence of the computer program they had themselves patented, Columbine's own workforce too had lost the will to work.

The only exception to this was Marvin Halsteed himself; he had lost the will to work shortly after purchasing his first Rolls Royce some ten years earlier. So that made bugger all difference to anything. Indeed, with almost unimaginable wealth already secure in private accounts in Switzerland, Halsteed had even found it too much effort to bank his company's extraordinary profits and instead kept the money at home under his rotating waterbed, thereby avoiding the hardship of going to a cashpoint. The company was on the verge of collapse.

This, then, was the situation when I was brought in to provide the services of my vast knowledge and immense cerebral prowess. And apply it I did. Possessing a brain the size, power and, due to a childhood accident, shape of Macintosh Powerbook, I have never had to resort to a computer to solve my problems. Computer games are anathema to me, and I was therefore immune to the lure of the "Playsafe"™ system. Clearheaded, unlike the workshy, pixel-numbed morons surrounding me, I set about an analysis of the company's dilemma.

A fundamental tenet of business technique is that problems, when encountered, are not to be thought of merely as problems. They are also *opportunities*. If a man loses his arm in a mangling machine, he may no longer be able to be work or provide a living for himself or his family; but on the other side of the coin, that man will be able to walk through narrower doorways than the rest of us. When he is meeting important people, he will never have to worry about whether his fingernails are clean. Similarly, if a woman is hit by a bus, she may have horrific injuries, but she has also gained an insight into the physical properties of bus-fronts. Perhaps, if she put her mind to it, she could design a new bus-front that was less painful to be hit by.

In this particular instance the *problem* was Columbine's, but the *opportunity* was mine: opportunity to reap enormous profit for myself. Whilst the management and staff of Columbine were fumbling about in their amateur, dreamlike way, I went straight to the heart of the problem. In order to survive, Columbine needed to increase their sales. As they saw it, that required a reversal of the industrial decline of the nation as a whole. As this had proved beyond the power of successive post-war governments of both left and right, they believed that there was little they could do in this regard. (How different it could have been if I had won the Crulton by-election of 1975 for the Conservatives and taken my rightful place on the front benches. Sadly I was denied the opportunity. During the campaign, the Labour candidate asked me to consult on his best method of winning the seat, which had been in safe Tory hands since 1912. Unable to resist the challenge, I decided to proffer him false advice and suggested that he launch a personal attack upon my good self, painting me as ignorant, pompous and unfit for parliament. I felt that such a scurrilous tactic would doom the ploy to failure, and guarantee that I be returned as Member. Imagine my upset when his speeches seemed to strike a chord amongst the local populace and he took Crulton, overturning an 18,000 majority with a swing of 98%.)

In any event, without my help, those in governmental power seemed to be making a right old hash of it and any change in our industrial fortunes seemed highly unlikely. This, then, was not the solution for Columbine Software. Another route would be required. In the end it turned out to be quite simple. It would not be necessary to rely on the UK market if new outlets could be found abroad. I found it hard to believe that laziness is a purely British phenomenon. Certainly my Filipino houseboy works hard when I am in the house, but as soon as I have left? There are days when, on my return home, I am painfully aware from his sleepy demeanour that he has only just slipped into the gingham dress and pinny that I require him to wear.

So, Columbine was neglecting its markets abroad; but this was only half the solution. Any export of the product would surely cripple the overseas economies, forcing them into as parlous a state as our own. If this export-drive were coupled with a total ban on "Playsafe"™ within this country, the British economy would quickly recover its former might. Reverse takeovers would surely follow. Britain would become the most powerful industrial nation in the world, and if my consultancy fee were based on a percentage of Columbine's sales, and my role in the process became known and rewarded accordingly, I would become the most powerful man in the country, and then the world.

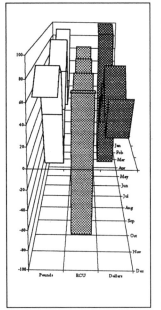

An incomprehensible graph

To me it was clear. But to those fumbling nobodies? Still, they were as putty in my hands.

The exportation of "Playsafe"™ was to be no problem. Columbine had agents and distributors all over the world, although "Playsafe"™ had never been among their list of products. The intention had always been that it would be an international program, but when the time had come to implement the plan the sales department had been absorbed in a game of Donkey Kong and had forgotten to do it.

The most likely spanner in the works would be getting the government ban on the product in the UK. The program itself was already being used by all government departments except Agriculture and Fisheries, who, being a bunch of farmers, had no idea how to use computers anyway. Worse still, the Chancellor of the Exchequer was so addicted to the software that he had just won through to the finals of Gamesmaster. (A ridiculous cover-story about ERM entry and interest-rate disagreements had to be invented to explain his eventual resignation.)

In the end, I calculated that what was needed to guarantee the ban was nothing less than the blackmailing of a senior government official.

It is always crucial to focus precisely upon what you want to achieve, although becoming the most powerful man in the world is, I am sure you will agree, quite a broad goal. However, it was with this clearly in mind that I cut through the wires to the alarms and security cameras of No 10 Downing Street one evening late in December 1990. My plan was simple. Below me, on the drainpipe, was my houseboy dressed only in crotchless panties and a black Gossard wonderbra. Above us lay the window of the new Prime Minister's bedroom. In my hand I held a Canon SLR with autofocus and built-in flash. I thought two pictures would do it. Threatened with these being sent to a major national newspaper, I estimated that the PM would force through the ban in the next session of parliament. Sadly, however, it was not to be. The drainpipe snapped, my houseboy fell into the Downing Street garden with an inappropriately loud thud and those constables normally stationed at the front of the building appeared at the rear.

Once arrested, one is checked on the National Crime Computer, which attempts to match your physical characteristics with those of listed criminals, in order to see if you are wanted for any other misdemeanour. I knew for certain, having never been in such a situation before, that my name would not appear, and was also confident that, with my near-infinite wealth and immense power, I would be immune from prosecution. I had however reckoned without "Playsafe"™. When checking my data, the operator of the police computer forgot which screen he was looking at and, being short and mustachioed, I was taken into custody on suspicion of being a SuperMario Brother.

CASE-STUDY TWO:

H.M. PRISON ROUGHLEY

I became involved with Roughley late in December 1990, when I was asked by Her Majesty's Government to stay there for a period of two months, whilst I was awaiting trial. It was a period of intensive consultancy opportunities, for apart from the occasional visit to London in a high-security van, in order to attend various hearings relating to my case, I spent the entire sojourn within the establishment. Indeed, even the visits to London provided scant relief, my desire to see old friends being rather curtailed by the impossibility of seeing anything when you have a blanket over your head.

The problem facing Roughley was this. Britain's prisons had all been built in the nineteenth century when the idea of punishment for prisoners took sway over that of penal reform. Prisoners were incarcerated to repay their debt to society, and whether or not they emerged better people was of no interest. Prisons were therefore dank, dark and forbidding places with few amenities or comforts for their inmates. They had also been designed to hold roughly half the number of inmates they were now catering for; in short they were both overcrowded and outmoded.

The obvious answer was to create more space and more amenities by expanding the prisons.

However, a building programme would cost money, and, being a non-commercial concern, each prison would either have to justify the expenditure to central government, or raise the money itself. This, then, was the task facing me.

Fortunately in this task I was not to be alone, for shortly after my arrival I discovered that Sir Albert Arbitrage and Sir Stuart Leverage-Buyout, former Chairman and Chief Executive respectively of Fraudster Corporation, had also been seconded to the establishment. Sir Albert was on a five-year project and Sir Stuart on two three-year assignments which were to run concurrently. They too were extremely concerned about the general level of overcrowding, especially amongst members of the business establishment who were trying to combine their visit with the running of a corporation on the outside. Overcrowding was severely hampering their ability to do this successfully. In some cases convicted businessmen were three to a cellphone.

I agreed that this was an outrage and we decided to join forces, combining my genius with their modest talent, in order to solve the central problem: too many prisoners in too small a space. I also believed that a successful outcome to the problem might guarantee me an early release and allow me to get back to the problem of Columbine and my plans for world domination, which I had had to put on hold for the duration. Alternatively, it might ease a transfer to Parkhurst where I could be reunited with my Filipino houseboy, the vision of whose night-time attire was filling an increasing number of my waking moments.

We decided initially upon a meeting with the governor in order to assess the strength of the management structure. The governor's office is high up in the central prison block, overlooking the high-security wing, there positioned so that those prisoners incarcerated in it are constantly aware of his authority. Unfortunately the windows of his office were also within range of the potties full of excreta that the high-security prisoners would fling from their cells in order to show him how much respect they had for the authority of which he was representative. For a long time the governor had been hell-bent upon retaliation. He had toyed with taking away their privileges, but remembered just in time that they didn't have any in the first place. He had toyed with reducing the number of visits allowed them, but remembered that they were not allowed any of those either. In his blackest moments, when his brain was particularly addled, or a fresh potty had just landed on his freshly cleaned glass, he shouted at them that if they did not stop, he would put them all in solitary confinement, which, frankly, is not much of a threat to someone who is already in solitary confinement. Eventually he decided that the only retribution he could take would be to go into their cells and scratch out the little marks on the wall that told them how long they had been in there. Petty, but immensely satisfying. In the longer term, however, he needed to find a way of putting physical distance between himself and his tormentors. We therefore surmised that he might be amenable to any means of accomplishing the building of a new wing.

When sitting in one's leather Chesterfield chair, behind one's Georgian desk, in the oak-panelled chairman's office, down the oak-panelled corridor, at the end of a long, impressive and ludicrously remunerative career, it is difficult to believe that anything should or will ever change. This is especially so if one is chairman. After all, by the time the company reaps the benefits of your incisive and far-reaching decisions, you will have left to enjoy a long and splendid retirement at your country mansion. It will be of little concern to you whether your former employers are using the most up to date potash feeder, have split their ball-bearing business into two separate divisions in order to achieve internal competition, or have built a new chocolate-wrapper plant on the banks of a local river, so as to exploit both the regional transport hub and the fact that if you dump all the waste into the river the local council is unlikely to prosecute you. For you will no longer be there to enjoy the benefits of such changes. Your mind will be occupied with much more trivial matters such as which major world capital to spend the weekend in, or whether to buy an eighth Range Rover. The implementation of change should, therefore, be left in the hands of the junior management who are still hungry and willing to get their hands dirty.

We were therefore surprised at the response we received to our suggestions from the governor. Firstly, let me put him in his correct context. Here was a man who lived in a small terraced house, built of the same depressing grey stone as the rest of the prison. A man who earned next to nothing, and could afford even less. In short, a loser with much to gain from the implementation of change. Why, then, did he react so unfavourably to our proposals? To us the situation was completely clear. The best course would be to gain government support for the building programme. To this end we suggested to the governor a rooftop protest. We even suggested ourselves as the main protagonists: the sight of two knights of the realm, barechested, throwing roof slates at passing policemen and warders, would be certain to increase media interest in the issue of overcrowding. Of course, the publicity generated might also produce further consulting work for Sir Albert, Sir Stuart and myself, but there is no harm in a little self-publicity. Indeed, Sir Stuart had already begun work on a long banner made out of sheets, reading "Rooftop protest organised by Bradford Swingely...", which we were planning to use for the benefit of the television cameras.

As soon as we tabled this proposal, the governor called for two more warders to be brought into the room. Initially we imagined this was so that they too could marvel at our business prowess and the breadth of our thinking, and we were therefore somewhat surprised when it emerged that they were there to escort us back to our quarters. Indeed, Sir Albert seemed not to understand at all, and only became clear on the issue when one arm was bent forcibly behind his back, the other pulled across his own neck, and he was asked by the hairiest of the warders, who seemed to assume that he was very shortsighted indeed, whether he would like to take a closer look at the Governor's marble mantelpiece.

Do you know what it is yet?

We have all been in meetings where our arguments did not meet with the desired response. This has happened to me often as my thinking tends to be so far in advance of other men, my vision so great, that it is almost incomprehensible. Leonardo was in much the same position of course, although I feel my case to be more extreme. Had I lived at the time of Da Vinci, the world would not have been left a drawing of a flimsy wooden helicopter but would have been bequeathed a fully functional vertical-take-off Harrier at the very least. When I am at the very peak of my capabilities I sometimes feel, perhaps slightly arrogantly, that compared to the laser-like precision of my thought processes, Einstein himself was merely wrestling with

141

fog. Being surrounded by lesser men is a cross I have to bear, but it does not make me unsympathetic to their cerebral shortcomings. Sometimes if a lesser mortal has failed to grasp my ideas at the first attempt I will repeat them again, more slowly. If this does not work I repeat them for a second time, at the same speed, but more loudly. If this does not work, I will quite simply deride them for their base stupidity. This, of course, does nothing to help them understand the points at issue, but it makes me feel a whole lot better.

As I was being propelled towards the door of the governor's office, I attempted to use all these techniques but am ashamed to say that none of them made the slightest difference, except perhaps the last which, if anything, accelerated our ejection and may have something to do with the fact that my memory of the incident ends at that point, and recommences with being awakened in the hospital sickbay.

Thinking back, it was obvious that in the governor and his staff we had come across a conservative management structure which would stand little chance of survival if exposed to the vagaries of commercial competition. We had moved too far and too fast for them. We would therefore have to look at the second possible solution: that of raising the money for the building programme ourselves.

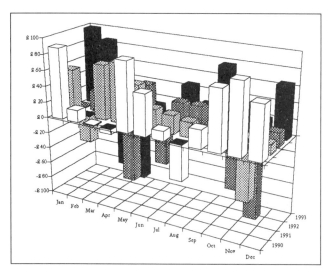

I have no idea what this refers to

Often an organisation will under-utilise its human resources, and this appeared to be exactly what had happened at Roughley. No-one, it seemed, had asked the prisoners themselves how they would go about raising money, in spite of the fact that many of them had excellent ideas to offer. Over the course of three weeks Sir Stuart, Sir Albert and I set out to put this straight with a series of consultative meetings, held in our cells. The ideas put forward were both interesting and in some cases radical, proving once again that the desire for change will come from below if it is allowed to. Already areas of the prison itself were highly entrepreneurial. One inmate, Barry "Madhead" McRea, was running several small businesses within our wing. The most successful of these was a small security firm, which guaranteed the safety of any inmate from the extreme and unbridled violence of McRea and his cohorts as long as a small payment was made to McRea himself at the end of each week. This seemed to us a perfect business. There were no costs of production, no stock-control problems, and a guaranteed supply of customers, whether they wanted to be customers or not.

I was also impressed by McRea. Like most good managers, he seemed to enjoy his work and also cared for the well-being of his customers, as I was to find out. Having joined the scheme myself, and having paid my fee not to receive the product, which was in this case the knuckleduster-clad hand of his chief executive, Jock "Howitzer" McTavish, he gave it to me anyway. As he explained, generosity is a good

142

way of keeping customers happy, and he aimed on average to beat one in four of his customers shitless every week, even if they had paid their dues.

McRea also ran an importation business, which operated at the regular visiting sessions for the inmates. Again, it was simple and well organised. The various wives or girlfriends of the inmates would bring with them whatever illegal drugs they had procured since their last visit. McRea would then distribute these to his customers throughout the prison, always being careful to keep some back to give to new customers whom he was hoping to wean on to the various substances. Normally he would restrict this activity to new, young, long-stay prisoners, thereby maintaining his customer-base for years to come.

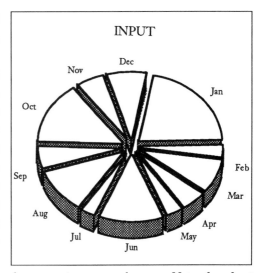

This business worried me deeply for, unlike the security arm, the importation business had no control over supply, which it seemed to me could cease at any time. Indeed, in the past there had been unfortunate breaks in the availability of such drugs, which had caused some problems due to the excessive number of inmates walking about shivering, drenched with sweat and moaning. I therefore suggested to McRea that the manufacture of these drugs be brought in-house, so such shortfalls would not occur again. He replied that to his way of thinking, the uncertainty of supply was a lesser evil than the certainty of discovery, called me a "soft southern git" and smashed a brick into my face.

Although highly successful in themselves, both McRea's businesses suffered from the problem of a captive market of finite size. If the building programme were to be self-funding it would have to generate more money than either of these ventures could hope to raise alone. McRea, however, had another idea which could fit the bill. He knew, having tortured me mercilessly in the communal washing area with a piece of lead piping and a frayed rope, that the former Chairman of Columbine Software, Marvin Halsteed, had never used banks and kept the company's entire profits, a sum in excess of £14 million, beneath his water-bed.

It was his intention to deprive Mr Halsteed of this cash and divert it to Roughley, where it could be used to rebuild the main block, including a personal, marble-lined penthouse apartment for McRea. Sir Albert and Sir Stuart were enthusiastic about the idea from the word go. Such a sum would easily pay for a new high-security wing and more besides. I was less certain. My agreement was, however, quickly secured by the application of a corkscrew to my genitalia by the dangerously alcoholic "Howitzer". I was also somewhat afraid that, if I were to refuse involvement, McRea would cut off the supplies of heroin to which I had now become addicted.

The first management problem to be confronted was how to gain the freedom to carry out the burglary. One of us, at least, would have to be on the outside to organise it. My penis being deep in argument with a rusty crown-corker that "Howitzer" McTavish was wielding, in the belief that my reproductive organ was a bottle of continental bottled lager, I suggested that I be the one to undertake this difficult task, and not wishing to run the risk of an actual escape, with the dodging of large, dentally-gifted dobermans that this involved, I began to think of alternative methods of release. Surely a "white-collar" inmate like myself, if deranged in a non-violent way, would be sent to a slightly less secure establishment. Indeed, if one were seriously mad, one would almost certainly be released into the community to save money and allowed to wander around with no supervision at all, required to sleep in shop doorways and annoy passengers on the top deck of buses by talking to non-existent friends. This then became my plan.

It was at this point that I demanded to be taken to the governor's office. I was, I explained, a lampstand, and my 60-watt bulb had just blown.

What the fuck does this mean?

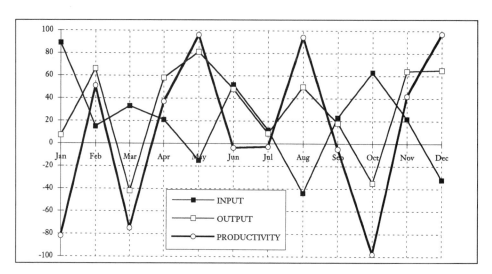

CASE-STUDY THREE:

OUTSIDE DIXONS PLC

My association with the doorway of Dixons, on the Strand, London, began shortly after I thrust my fingers into a three-pin socket at H.M. Prison Roughley. My problem is this. Everybody thinks that I'm mad. But I'm not. I'm just a perfectly ordinary light fitting. Screw-type bulb, of course, not one of those bayonet things. Don't worry, I'm just pretending to be mad so I can get out and get all that money. Osram are my favourite, I think, although I have had some very good Philips soft-focus. Sometimes, pretending to be mad can drive you a bit funny in the head, but not me. Ethel agrees with me. She is the daughter of Rameses the Second, and when I'm rich she's going to help me rule the world. No-one works any more, you know. This Dixons is all closed up now, since they banned computer games. I'm sure I thought of doing that, but seems they have given all the credit to Sir Ivan Gobbscheidt, Knight of the Realm, Chairman of Columbine and prize bastard. I wonder if he wants any business advice. I'll give him some. Piss off, Scumbag!!!!!! I might go to Manila soon, get myself a Filipino houseboy. Do you want to change my bulb?

144

ROYALTY

"As serialized in a leading Sunday newspaper, and criticized by all the others who pretended they hadn't bid for it."

DAVINA

Her Untrue Story

ANDREW MARTIN

the extortionate cover price of the hardcover version of
Davina: Her True Story caused a worldwide sensation.
Now it is available in paperback at a slightly lower price.

Get yourself to the cash till and buy one.

FOREWORD

The biggest problem facing royal writers is that of authenticity. The private life of the Royal Family is cloaked in mystery. Those closest to them are sworn to protect their secrets and to defend the family from the unwanted intrusion of journalists. Few interviews are given and even then one cannot help but wonder whether one is being told the whole truth, or a watered down version of it – a cover or shield to prevent the real facts emerging.

This biography, however, does not suffer from such difficulties. It was written entirely independently of Buckingham Palace, and is free from the unwanted attention of the Royal Press Office. Most importantly of all, it makes no attempt to be accurate. It is possibly the worst researched book ever to be written about the House of Windsor, relying on a handful of personal reminiscences from people who have probably never even met the Royal Family. In short, it is a pack of lies.

INTRODUCTION

They are the main tourist attraction in modern-day Britain if you don't count Alton Towers or the British Museum. Their faces fill the pages of thousands of magazines throughout the world. The slightest whiff of scandal in their midst banishes news of natural disasters, economic downturns and sporting triumphs from newspaper headlines throughout the world. They are the Royal Family, the House of Windsor, the ruling house of the United Kingdom of Great Britain and Northern Ireland. The family of Queen Elizabeth the Second, the titular head of state not only of these islands, but of Australia, and New Zealand, and lots of other places that play cricket rather better than we do. The Falkland Islands, for example.

The image of the sovereign is ubiquitous on stamps and coins and banknotes. There cannot be one person alive in Britain today who does not recognise her characteristic profile, specifically designed to make her look thirty years younger than she actually is. But how much do we really know about her and her family? How much do we know of what goes on behind the closed doors of the royal palaces at Sandringham or Balmoral? What do we know of Highgrove, or Hampton Court? And what of Buckingham Palace? We know that when the flag is flying high above the Mall the monarch is in residence, but this is where certainty ends and we dive off into the shady netherworld of speculation and rumour. Or at least this book does, as it tells the story of Lady Davina Spenthrood.

CHAPTER ONE:
Sniffing the Trail

As I sat in my bedsit that fateful afternoon, mindlessly waiting for the start of *Blockbusters,* nothing could have prepared me for the phone call I was about to receive. After nearly three months working as the court reporter for the *East Midlands Exclaimer*, I believed that I had an almost unparalleled knowledge and understanding of the workings of the British monarchy. My contacts were wide-ranging and more than willing to talk to me on an exclusive basis, knowing how sympathetically I would listen to the stories they had to tell, and the frankly over-generous manner in which I would brandish my cheque book.

Yet even I was shocked by what I was told that day. Shocked by the real-life drama that lay behind the serene facade of Kensington Palace. Shocked by the actual state of the most popular of Royal marriages. Shocked by the true story of the Prince of Wales and Lady Davina Spenthrood.

Looking back, I should have known that something was amiss. Only three months earlier I had had my first glimpse of the private face of the House of Windsor. Indeed, I had even written an article about it, "The Royal Flag Saga", for the *Exclaimer.*

According to Royal lore, when the monarch is in residence a flag is raised above Buckingham Palace. It is a tradition stretching back to the time of Edward the Seventh, a king very keen on naval signalling who used to raise a whole selection of flags spelling out various messages. People boating in St James's Park were often alarmed to see a signal flying from the Palace reading, "German Gunboat in vicinity. Be on Guard", or, "Do not approach. Suspected Yellow Fever". The latter signal was to prove a useful deterrent if the crowds for the Changing of the Guard looked as though they might swell to unmanageable proportions. His favourite, however, was a missive to his mistress (whose apartments overlooked nearby Hyde Park Corner) which read, "Mrs Langtry, the Queen is out. I wish to be in. I want you now", often to be followed by a second message, "Wear your stockings. It's Shagtime".

In modern times, however, a single Union Jack flies when the monarch is in residence. Whenever she leaves it is pulled down and whenever she returns it is raised once more. As such it is a surefire indicator of comings and goings at the palace, and an uncanny thermometer for the temperature of the Royal marriage. In recent months it had been going up and down like a yoyo. On one day in March 1991, the Royal Flag raisers, of whom my inside source was one, had had to raise the flag no fewer than fourteen times, as the monarch continually stormed out of the Palace after arguing with her spouse over his habit of playing the bazouki in their bedroom, and leaving half-eaten boxes of Marks and Spencer moussaka on top of the television set.

Although the arguments ceased when the Queen threatened to move in with her mother, this wasn't before the flag raisers had presented a petition to the sovereign demanding that they be provided with a new lightweight nylon flag, which would not only be much easier to pull up, but would also be easier to wash and require no ironing. The Queen turned the request down on the grounds that the static electricity from the nylon might affect the TV aerial and disrupt the reception of *Neighbours*, but after further lobbying eventually agreed to replace the old canvas Union Jack with an electrically neutral, cotton-rich polyester mix which could be placed in the tumble drier with no risk of shrinkage.

Even though I knew of the problems in the more senior of the Royal marriages, I still found it hard to believe what I was being told over the phone that afternoon: a marriage crumbling, the likelihood of a Royal divorce, the undue influence of a delicatessen assistant upon the heir to the throne. It all seemed hideously beyond the bounds of possibility, so, doubting the authenticity of my source, I agreed to meet him face to face.

Two days later, sitting opposite my informer in a pub in the Old Kent Road, and armed only with my cheque book, all my doubts were washed away. Quite apart from the story he was to tell me, his own life itself would make compelling reading. Prior to entering Royal Service he had spent four years in a Italian prison for forging and attempting to sell the diaries of Benito Mussolini to *Il Corriere della Sera*. It was something of which he was immensely proud, for the fraud had come perilously close to succeeding. In order to escape detection he had only used paper manufactured in 1927 at a small Italian paper mill in the village next to Mussolini's childhood home. He had immersed himself in the life and interests of the dictator and had developed a handwriting style indistinguishable from "Il Duce" himself. It was only pressure of time that had caught him out. Hounded by *Il Corriere* for the fifth and final instalment, he decided to cut a few corners and type out all the remaining diary entries on a Toshiba T2000SX Laptop, using Word for Windows 2.0c. Thinking this a little strange, Italian experts had tested the ink for age and found it to come from a Hewlett Packard Deskjet 500 Bubble Jet printer. Significantly, this model had not been available in Southern Italy in 1945 and the game was up.

Here, then, was an entirely trustworthy man with intimate Royal connections. The story you read here is largely as told to me that night, authenticated where necessary by talking to some of his mates and others who might know a bit about it. It is the story of Davina.

CHAPTER TWO:
"Gun For Your Wife"

When interviewed in the early 1970s, the Prince of Wales claimed that he would marry before the age of thirty. It was a prediction the press were to remember and as he approached the start of his fourth decade the search for a future queen became a national pastime. The press and public alike were clamouring for a royal marriage and the subsequent birth of a royal heir.

As his thirtieth birthday drew ever closer, the Prince formed and broke off liaisons with increasing frequency. In the space of eighteen months he courted Anna Montcrief de Montmorency Tugboat Dobson, daughter of the Fifth Earl of Credence, Ursula Porthole Stewart, and Emilia Corquindale McTavish Smythe, the daughter of a Scottish landowner, whom he had met whilst fishing for salmon on the River Tweed. The couple were literally thrown together by the explosion from some dynamite that the Prince had thrown into the water to alleviate the boredom of using a line.

Yet none of these liaisons held his interest. One, however, was to prove more lasting. On a trip into Beccles, from the family home in Sandringham, the Prince had popped, by chance, into the local Gateway where he had met and fallen in love with Jacinta Packball, a shop assistant who worked on the deli counter. It was an obsessive love. For a period of several months the Prince did not let her out of his sight, which increasingly conflicted with his royal duties. Official engagements were cancelled at short notice with the lamest of excuses. On one occasion the prince pulled out of a state visit to Kenya saying he had to visit Beccles to purchase taramasalata, smoked ham and vegetable samosas for the annual gathering of the Order of the Garter at Windsor.

Eventually he would only accept engagements if Jacinta could come along too. That summer he took her on the 35-day Royal visit to Australia, which was to cause further problems. Having used twelve days of her holiday entitlement at Christmas, visiting the Royal Family at Balmoral, Jacinta could not get official leave for the whole trip. Eventually a compromise was reached whereby Gateway allowed her to go as long as she worked while she was there. A mobile delicatessen was installed on the Royal Yacht Britannia, from which Jacinta sold a selection of cold meats and pasties to all the dignitaries and heads of state who came aboard. So successful was she that even Paul Keating, the anti-royalist Australian politician, found himself buying four different types of olive and half a kilo of hoummos. Jacinta soon became internationally famous, and girls the world over started to follow her fashion example. From London to New York teenagers began to wear the dark green shop coat of the Gateway chain, put their hair in a bun and sport the see-through, aerated plastic gloves that Jacinta had made her own. Soon, even the traditional calling card bowed to the trend for all things "Jacinta", being replaced by small paper raffle tickets with "your number in the queue" printed at the top.

It was, however, a romance doomed to failure. A national newspaper received information that Jacinta had had a previous relationship, albeit shortlived, with the non-foods/household goods manager of the Gateway superstore in Saxmundham. Despite the fact that he had had hundreds of illicit liaisons, the Prince was devastated and the relationship ended abruptly, putting paid to a marriage that seemed to have become a near certainty.

Other relationships were no more successful. Like many men the Prince was constantly attracted to women who looked like members of his own family, but he was to fall foul even of this, when, during a trip to Ascot, he fell head over heels in love with "Curragh's Pride", the winner of the previous year's Derby.

Again, marriage seemed a distinct possibility and there are those who believe that a proposal was actually made. Unfortunately, wishing to follow the Prince's example, the horse too went down on one knee, a movement to which it was not anatomically suited, broke its leg and had to be put down.

The Prince also cast his net overseas, searching out eligible Royal princesses. This again was to prove problematic, for most of the Royal houses of our European neighbours were overthrown and deprived of their wealth during the nineteenth century. As a result, a continental aristocrat might merely hold title rather than position, as the Prince was to find out, when, the morning after having dinner with Marie-Anne, Princess Royal of the Grand Duchy of Luxembourg, she knocked on the door of his hotel room to find out if it was convenient to clean it yet.

The Prince reached the lowpoint in this flurry of relationships when he started courting Ethel Breedmarsh, a bag lady he had met on the forecourt of Waterloo Station who claimed to be the daughter of Pharaoh Rameses the Second. Her regal credentials seemed impeccable. Not only was she a direct descendant of the Royal Family of ancient Egypt, but she also claimed to be personally acquainted with Charles the First and Ethelred the Unready, having lived with both of them in a hostel in Camden Town.

Again, the relationship was intense. The Prince became a regular visitor to the hostel and, for the month or so that it lasted, was often to be seen sitting in the doorway of the Camden branch of the London Electricity Board, clutching a can of Tennants Extra and chatting to his newfound friends.

Then, one weekend, late in the summer of 1978, the situation was to change dramatically. The Prince met Lady Davina Spenthrood. The occasion was the now-famous shooting party at the Sussex home of their mutual friends the Terter-Terter Tomkinson Himmlers. Archie Terter-Terter Tomkinson Himmler was an eminent speech therapist, specialising in helping those with stutters. The key to his success was the confidence he imparted to sufferers, who finding that they could pronounce their therapist's name, first time, with no difficulty whatsoever, quickly overcame their problem entirely. The Prince had known the family since childhood and had spent several years under Archie's professional guidance in an attempt to overcome his own speech difficulty – an inability to open his mouth without sounding like someone struggling valiantly to jettison waste products in the absence of sufficient dietary fibre. In short, whenever the Prince spoke in public he would put a straining, strangulated "eeeer..." at the start of each word, an impediment that tended to distract the audience from the points he was trying to make. After one particularly heartfelt speech to the Association of British Motor Vehicle Manufacturers in which he rued the waning of classical architectural principles in car design and suggested the inclusion of Hermes, Caryatids and Corinthian pillars in place of the standard doorstays on the Austin Allegro, one commentator wrote, "Closing one's eyes, it was as if one were in a public lavatory listening to the incoherent ramblings of a constipated lunatic struggling in the cubicle next door."

What is more, the impediment was extremely time-consuming and every speech the Prince made became almost twice its optimum length, leaving audiences caught between the devil and the deep blue sea: consciousness and terminal boredom or unconsciousness and imaginative transportation to that rather unpleasant civic amenity of which the commentator had written. Instead of the six or seven official engagements carried out every day by other members of the Royal Family, the Prince was only managing two at the absolute maximum. The Press had duly noted that his workload was the lowest of any Royal and had begun to question his right to the funds he received from the Civil List.

Archie Terter-Terter Tomkinson Himmler had tried every technique at his disposal, but the Prince seemed unable to overcome his problem. Eventually it was decided that the best course would be to try and sidestep the impediment by incorporating it into the actual formation of his words. Speeches were written for the Prince containing as many words as possible beginning with "er", and the Prince began to choose his areas of special interest with this technique in mind. He accepted the presidency of the Royal Society of Eeer..gonomics, spoke at the Eeer...th Summit, and became Secretary of the British branch of the Eeer..tha Kitt Fan Club. For a while this appeared to work. Speeches became shorter and the Palace even considered removing the words "Please Bring Pro-Plus – Lots of it – and a Book or Something" from the invitations to events at which the Prince was to speak.

It was not long, however, before he was back to his old habits, and soon even the fact that many of the words in his speeches began with "eeer" did not stop him from putting "eeer" in front of them anyway. Eventually the problem became so bad that he would not only put an "eeer" at the start of the word, but would insert them randomly throughout. Fearing professional embarrassment that could cost him his career, Archie – or Eeer..Arch..eeer..ie..eeer, as the Prince called him – referred his patient to another eminent practitioner in the field, Sir Murdo McMuffin, whose technique was rather less subtle. Every time the Prince uttered the offending sound, Sir Murdo would place the Royal testes in a mangle. Again this treatment was to backfire, for all it did was to make the Prince continue to emit the offending noise, but in a somewhat higher register.

Lady Davina's connection with the family was slightly less obscure. Her mother, Lady Clarissa Boothby-Bloodhound, was a colourful character who had been a leading light of the London social scene in the 1940s. A female racing driver, she was the darling of the crowds at Brooklands as, seemingly unaware of the immense danger to life and limb, she took the steeply banked turns at near impossible speed, appearing to defy gravity itself on the most hair-raising corners. Her driving was in many ways a mirror of her personality: courageous, craving excitement and immensely stupid. Many centuries of inbreeding amongst the Boothby-Bloodhounds had left her with a brain the size of a cocktail cherry, and in spite of a record 153 lessons with the British School of Motoring, which Lady Clarissa claimed totalled only 99 because she couldn't count any further, she had never quite grasped what the brakes did, or indeed where they were. Approaching a bend, and thinking she had located the elusive pedal, she would press down on it as hard as she could, only to produce a massive surge of acceleration, drawing gasps of appreciation from the crowd. At the end of the race the only way she could guarantee bringing the car to an absolute halt was to aim at the stacked bales of hay that lined the track, close her eyes and pray. Generally the technique worked, but at the Spring race meeting of 1943, hampered by an eye infection and travelling at unparalleled speed, she had aimed for some rather small, very tightly stacked russet-coloured bales, and drove straight into the main supporting wall of the Brooklands Clubhouse. Both her Bugatti "Diabolo" six-cylinder and her short career came to an abrupt halt. Although no longer able to drive, she still craved excitement, and so turned to the slightly more sedate, though no less thrilling, pastime of gambling. It was through this that she became acquainted with Archie's father, the fifth Earl of Maltby, for in the summer of 1948 he held a house party at his Sussex residence, the imaginatively named Maltby Hall, to which Lady Clarissa was invited, the Earl having heard of her fondness for cards. Every evening she would play with her host and, due to her own inability to count or even identify different suits, had soon run up an unmanageable debt. A deal had therefore been struck whereby her children, as yet unborn, would go into the Earl's service until they achieved their majority at the age of twenty-one.

Thus, just two days after her birth, Lady Davina was sent to join her brother and older sister at Maltby Hall where they were pressed into service in the kitchens and on the home farm. It was a life they enjoyed, largely because they had nothing to compare it with. Although they longed to see their mother, Lady Clarissa barely kept in touch with any of her children. This was partly due to a basic lack of maternal feelings, but

153

Ascot. Davina's lady-in-waiting, Marilyn Ffinchley-Central, desparately tries to find the toilet

Davina on a family holiday, 1963. She looks understandably nervous. With good reason, as it turned out

DAVINA

The "black sheep of the family" – Davina's uncle, the Earl of Dorking, in Pall Mall

Davina's ex-flatmate Melissa Dredfly-Uppaclarse had a longstanding romance with an engineering student from Keele

In 1991, amateur radio-ham Reggie Prebble picked up a royal phone conversation totally by accident on his home-made apparatus, he did, honest. It definitely wasn't M.I.5 or anything

Davina's friend Caroline Aufley-Porshe married in 1984. She and her husband now model for British Home Stores

Her Untrue Story

Davina's great-aunt Belinda went senile. Eventually, she would only come ski-ing if told she was going to Eastbourne

Royal circles were shocked when Davina saw this photo and commented "I think Lenin had a point."

155

largely because she had lost count of how many offspring she actually had. Realising that she could offer them in lieu of debts, she had borne children every twelve months from the age of 21 to 56 and they were now spread around the globe, compensating for her shortcomings at gin rummy. Even today, living in Argentina, post-menopausal and on the run from the British fraud squad, she presses on with her unique method of debt repayment, either by inviting friends' children to come and stay for the weekend and then stealing them, or by encouraging her own children to reproduce and then using their offspring to satisfy the unshaven, be-sunglassed heavies who come knocking at her door.

That particular weekend, in the summer of 1978, Archie Terter-Terter Tomkinson Himmler had organised a shoot on the family estate in Sussex. Unfortunately, the day before, an air traffic controllers' strike had necessitated a change in the flight path to Gatwick Airport, such that it passed directly overhead, causing such a degree of noise pollution that all the birds had taken off to quieter climes. Left with nothing to shoot, Archie had taken drastic measures. Dressing Davina in camouflage green and forcing her to strap a pheasant to her head, he had sent her out into the undergrowth, with instructions to run from side to side very fast when she heard the shooting party approaching. This she had done, but not quite fast enough, for the Prince, who is renowned as one of the finest shots in the country, let loose from fifty yards and caught her a glancing blow to the head. She fell like a stone and, thinking he had bagged a pheasant, the Prince sent his gun dog to retrieve the bird.

To meet in such a way might not seem the most promising of starts, but as the Prince looked down on the bloodied, unconscious heap that the dog dumped at his feet, something stirred inside him. Under normal circumstances he would have been deeply upset that Davina had not curtsied or addressed him as "Sir", but on this occasion he found himself able to put that consideration aside, unusually moved to forgiveness by her gaping head wound and strangely twisted neck, which still bore the small red-raw puncture-marks of dog teeth.

Davina was dragged back to the house, where she was placed on the kitchen table in the servants' quarters. As soon as the shoot was over a doctor was called out to have a look at her. Fortunately nothing too serious was wrong. Catching her just above the ear, the shot had passed through her skull, coming within inches of her brain, which was thankfully slightly smaller than her mother's, before exiting through the cheekbone on the other side. After a swift examination it was decided that no visit to the hospital would be necessary and, finding a couple of bottles of Burgundy on the kitchen dresser, the doctor simply removed the corks and placed one in each of the holes on either side of her head, telling her to rest for a while, or at least until the bleeding ceased. This was more difficult to ascertain than might be imagined, there being some confusion as to whether the claret-coloured stains visibly spreading over the corks were blood or simply residual red wine.

When he returned to the house the Prince made it his business to find out how Davina was, sending one of his servants to the kitchen to have a look at her and, if necessary, cover her in a horse blanket. Only when he was satisfied that she was not yet dead did he settle down with the rest of the assembled company to enjoy the feast that his host had prepared for him.

Traditionally, the centrepiece of such a feast is the game that has been shot but unfortunately on this occasion none had been bagged. It was, therefore, a pleasant surprise for everyone, not least the Prince, when, as a replacement, the now partially conscious body of Lady Davina was brought out on a huge white porcelain serving dish, to serve as the focal point of the table setting. As she lay there, the Prince found he could not take his eyes off her and, in her numbed state, she too caught his gaze and returned it with her one functioning eyeball.

CHAPTER THREE:
A Fine Romance

It was by any standards an unusual romance. To begin with they conversed only by letter, as the Prince did not wish to put Davina off with his speech impediment before they had really had a chance to get to know each other. The arrangement was not altogether satisfactory. During the post-shoot feast Archie had forgotten that Davina was on the table for decorative purposes only and had taken a large slice from her arm with a carving knife. He realised his mistake as he was dipping the meat in redcurrant jelly, but by then it was too late; the damage had been done. The tendons of Lady Davina's right wrist had been severed and, for several months, writing with it was impossible. To write, she therefore had to use her left hand, which led the reader to speculate that the words had been written by a small child who should still really only be using crayons, as opposed to the small child just able to write with a biro that using her right hand would have suggested. Every letter to the Prince was a struggle and when they were strung together as words they were an impossibility.

Yet, despite these difficulties, the romance progressed and although they made every attempt to keep their feelings private, news of it soon reached the Press, who began mercilessly to hound Davina. Wherever she went the press pack would follow, asking her where she was going, what she felt about the Prince, whether the relationship was serious, and what the chances were of marriage. Often she simply ignored the questions and carried on her way, but more usually she did not understand the questions, particularly if they included long words like "and" or "if", and she would just smile sweetly back at the questioner.

Her life was changing radically. Having been ignored for years, she was suddenly invited to cocktail parties and receptions. Lord Maltby gave her a room in the Hall itself (although he did not help her to move her bedding from the stable), and relieved her of the most arduous of her duties. Even her mother began to take an interest in her, the possibility of marriage and offspring providing the potential solution to a rather large wager she had lost in Buenos Aires.

Soon things were happening at such a pace that Davina had no time left to think about her own feelings. In February 1979, just as the Press had been predicting for many months, the Prince proposed. It happened quite simply in the end. They had not seen each other since the weekend of the shooting party. He had been away in London with a hectic schedule of polo and cocktail parties that simply did not allow time for the sixty-mile drive down to Sussex to see her. They were, however, in regular telephone communication. Every week one of the Prince's equerries would phone Maltby Hall to find out how she was.

Davina did not altogether like the situation, but understood that there was very little alternative to this state of affairs. The Prince was very busy with the business of being future king, and she appreciated the time he spent telling one of his servants to enquire after her. In reality, though, she longed to see him and talk to him as most courting couples do. After all, apart from a brief glimpse, partially obscured by the feathers of the pheasant strapped to her head, and an moment of dazed semiconsciousness at the dinner table, during which there appeared to be at least three Princes all going round and round in a huge circle, she had never actually met him. To be honest, she was not at all sure that she could remember what he looked like, her only guide being a 1969 Prince of Wales investiture mug in which the Earl kept old paintbrushes, and on which the Prince's face was largely obscured by a circular blob of "Morning Sunrise" Dulux Weathershield.

Then one morning there came an envelope with a Buckingham Palace crest. Davina knew that it was something special as she had not received a letter since the very early days of their relationship, the telephone having replaced writing as their main means of communication. Eagerly she tore it open and as she read the contents her heart leapt, for inside was a proposal of marriage, dictated by the Prince and signed in his absence, a perforated tear-off reply form and a brown, second-class pre-paid envelope addressed to the Palace. She could barely believe it was happening, and for a few moments she merely stared at the simple typewritten question. "The Prince wishes to know if you will marry him?" and the command that followed it. "Please tick one of the boxes below."

Which should she fill in? "No. I will not marry the Prince" or "Yes. I will marry the Prince and renounce all rights to a private life." Suddenly she found herself picking up a pen and, breathing deeply in an attempt to steady herself, ticking in the affirmative. The rest of the form was less daunting and, having looked a few words up in a dictionary, including "supplementary", quickly filled in the supplementary questions, "Are you a virgin?" ("If No, please state when and how virginity was lost") and "Are your reproductive organs in fully working order?", ticking "yes" in both cases. Then she lovingly tore off the reply sheet and placed it in the envelope, ready for posting. Now all that was to be done was to wait the statutory twenty-eight days for her reply to be processed, after which she would receive official word from the Palace as to what the next step would be.

That night, as she lay in bed, she prayed fervently that her letter would not be lost or mislaid. She could not help but think of Princess Marianna of the Netherlands who had accepted a proposal of marriage from King Heinrich the Third by the same method. Sadly the form had been misdirected, ending up amongst replies to the annual Edam-waxing ceremony in the Hague and, by the time she had summoned up the courage to phone the palace to see what was going on some three months later, the King had made alternative arrangements, marrying

159

instead a cheesewaxer called Margarita whose reply to her profession's official gala had been similarly misdelivered.

In fact no such misfortune was to befall Davina. The Palace replied by return asking her be at St Paul's Cathedral on the morning of July 29th that year for the wedding ceremony. Enclosed with the letter was a map of London's bus and tube routes, with the nearest underground stop firmly underlined in biro.

Alternatively, she was told, she could get a cab, although she would have to pay for it out of her own pocket. She was also invited to Buckingham Palace the very next week for a brief meeting with her future husband.

Ironically, it was at this meeting with the Prince that her now well-chronicled eating difficulties began.

Over the preceding months Davina had developed an idealistic view of her husband, based on the image of him on the Maltby Investiture mug, but now, in the confines of the state dining-room at Buckingham Palace, she was confronted with the real thing. It was not so much the fact that neither his hair nor the left side of his face were bright yellow as she had been led to believe, that upset her, for although twelve years her senior the Prince was an attractive man. Polo, a regular fitness programme and yoga had kept him youthful, while his regular foreign trips had ensured a glowing, healthy tan. This gap between imagination and reality she could bridge happily, but what she found it impossible to come to terms with was the very thing he had feared all along might harm their relationship, namely the way he spoke.

The Prince had been in therapy with Sir Murdo McMuffin for five years by the time he met Davina, and had had his testes crushed more times than he cared to remember, but still there was no improvement in his speech impediment. Believing that the problem might actually be constipation rather than just sounding like it, he had even restricted his diet solely to All Bran and prunes, but to no avail. In fact the situation had deteriorated. Every word was still preceded by an appalling "eeer...", only now it was not simply the "eeer..." of the fibre-deficient, but the appalling "eeer..." of someone whose reproductive organs are being made two-dimensional. It was the awful searing cry of the animal caught in a trap, the grotesque wail of the mating vixen and the uncomprehending scream of the mourning mother rolled into one. And every time Davina heard it she wanted to throw up. At first it was possible to control the situation. If she made no attempt to talk to him, the Prince would remain silent and the problem was averted, but inevitably there came a point when he would open his mouth, perhaps just to talk to a servant and, in a reaction that was to become almost Pavlovian, she too would open hers and through it deposit the contents of her stomach.

At that first meeting she put the problem down to pre-wedding nerves, and hoped that she would overcome it as soon as they were married. It was to be a hope unfounded in reality.

Davina's discomfort was not caused purely by the Prince's impediment alone for, at that first lunch, it was made yet more acute by the identity of the royal waitress. Barely disguised beneath the staid black and white uniform, lurked the unmistakable form of Jacinta Packball. Davina had assumed that Jacinta was no longer part of the Prince's life, but as she watched her serve him lovingly with ham on the bone, Scotch eggs and a potato lathka, she suspected that theirs was a relationship that went beyond cold meat and vegetable delicacies. Whatever love they had felt for each other was clearly not yet extinguished.

Still, choosing to ignore what her own eyes and ears were telling her, as well as the large and smelly pile of semi-digested three-bean salad that lay on the table cloth in front of her, Davina pressed on with arrangements for the wedding.

July 29th was a glorious day, the sun shining unremittingly from a clear blue sky. An air of overwhelming happiness pervaded every corner of the capital. Wherever one looked were smiling faces, and even the birds seemed to join in the peal of bells as they rang loud and long from the dome of St Paul's Cathedral in expectation of the bride's arrival. Crowds thronged the streets, waving flags and singing as they waited for the bride to pass.

And a long wait it was. After much thought, Davina had decided upon the Central line and the short walk from St Paul's Underground station, as her best way of reaching the cathedral. Unfortunately the Palace had forgotten to tell her that in celebration of the marriage they had declared a public holiday and that the tubes would only be running a Sunday service. The short journey to the church from the Kensington house of Gemima Pilkington-Plasterboard, an old family friend to whom her younger brother Charles was enslaved, involved four changes of train and took just over three hours. One whole hour of this was taken up by the removal of a body from the line at Tottenham Court Road, the passenger in question having ironically lost the will to live after waiting an entire morning for a train to Ongar.

The delay in the ceremony was such that barely anyone actually saw it. In America, NBC eventually lost patience waiting for Davina to arrive and switched to a minor-league baseball game from Ohio, whilst in Sweden they could not allow the wedding to run over into coverage of their national herring filleting competition. In the end the only Europeans to see it at all were the French who, hearing that it was a debacle, and thus a chance to ridicule the British, decided at the last minute to change their schedules so it could be incorporated.

When they finally emerged from the cathedral at about 5.30 that evening to greet the six or seven people who had not either left through boredom or collapsed with heat exhaustion, the Prince and Davina looked to be a radiantly happy couple. Many still remember from newspaper photos the exquisitely happy look on Davina's face as her new husband directed her back to the tube, telling her, in a rare moment of intimacy, that if she was going to the Palace, she was better walking down to Ludgate Circus and getting the District line from Blackfriars. But it was not a happiness that was to last.

CHAPTER FOUR:

A Woman Alone

To the outside world Davina was incorporated painlessly, indeed happily, into the Royal Family. The whole nation rejoiced as one when she announced, just nine months after the wedding, that she was pregnant. Yet the truth of the matter was quite different. The couple did not even share a bed and had separate rooms at either end of the Palace. Indeed, the Prince had not even been present at the conception of his child, instead having an equerry deliver some Royal sperm and a basting syringe to Davina in her apartments.

As she now saw her husband more regularly, sometimes as often as once a week, Davina's eating problems became more acute and, unable to gain adequate nutrition, she began to lose weight noticeably. Worst of all, however, she became aware of the true measure of influence exerted over her husband by Jacinta Packball. One evening, knowing that the Prince was out, and desperate to exploit the opportunity to eat something that she would not throw up, Davina had ventured into the Palace kitchens where she had come upon a monogrammed Pork Pie, bearing the inscription "PC loves JP". Next to it, identically embossed with shortcrust pastry was a Chinese spring roll cut into the shape of a heart and pierced by an arrow-shaped spear of asparagus, from the wounds of which there dripped taramasalata.

Davina longed to confront the Prince, but that would mean talking to him, so she remained silent, bearing the pain alone.

This pain has continued throughout their marriage, leaving Davina with the sole comfort of her children. But even they are far away, for during the wedding ceremony Lady Clarissa, bored with the wait, had laid a bet with the Queen of Tonga, next to whom she was sitting, on the exact moment Davina would enter the cathedral. Having never learned to tell the time and too stupid to realise this might be a drawback in such a wager, she lost and was unable to pay the £150,000 involved. Therefore, in the finest family tradition, as soon as William was born he was shipped off to that small kingdom in the South Seas, where he will remain until his twenty-first birthday, returning only then, suntanned, fit and excellent at seven-a-side rugby, to claim the British throne.

So Davina must face the future alone, strengthened perhaps by the fact that her true story has now been told.

"He made us laugh,
and he made us cry.
Sometimes both."

CLOWN
in the Dumps

STAN DOWNE

CHAPTER ONE:

Small Beginnings, Big Dreams

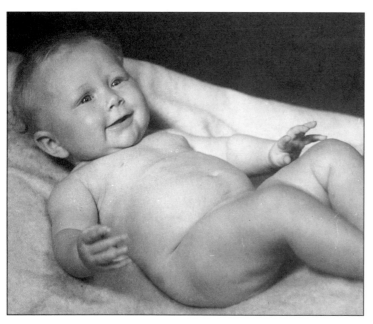

Me at two months. At this stage my parents were so poor, they could not afford to buy me a penis

I was born in 1920. I had a blissful, idyllic childhood, and my parents were wonderful. Nowadays, some of these actors and singers never seem to have a good word to say about their parents – can't wait to rush into print and say nasty things about them, doubtless for a large cheque. Well, I was brought up in a day when you were taught to respect your mother and father. If you didn't, they would belt you with a strap.

England was different then. It was cleaner, kinder, and gentler. Neighbours were neighbours. You could leave your front door open and no-one would burgle you. Everyone knew their place. Most of all – and I remember this very clearly – it was in black-and-white, and there was no sound.

We had no money. My father used to work eighteen hours a day down the mine, and at the end of a long day, he wasn't one of those who headed straight for the pub. He would come straight home to my mother. Since she was usually in the pub herself, I never understood this. We were so poor that, even with beer costing tuppence a pint, we could only afford six pints each, and one extra to put me to sleep.

I remember my father saying to me, "Sup up ale and get somnolent, lad." Father's hobby was words. He had a dictionary, his only book, that had been given to him by his father. He used to use lots of strange words from it. I think it was this that gave me my love of words. At school I used to long to get out of Pitdykewyke, but I remember our teacher, Mr Monkfish, telling me, "Tha's got big ideas, lad, but it's doon t'pit for you." I used to long to learn English literature, but the school only taught smelting and coking.

On Saturdays I used to go to the pictures in Cleckiemorple. I saw Buster Keaton, Laurel and Hardy, Chaplin, and the young Bob Monkhouse. I decided, as I sat in the 3d. seats, that I wanted to become an entertainer.

There was no show-business blood in our family at all apart from Uncle Simon, who had a dog act. He played the Northern music halls for a number of years. He based his act on a famous music-hall duo called Bombalini and his Perceptive Pooch. People in the audience would shout out sums and the dog would bark out the answers. For "two" he would give two barks, "seven" he would give seven barks, and so on. For more complex sums, a bark represented a whole number, a whimper represented "to the power of" and a low growl indicated a decimal point. In this way, over the years, Bombalini and his Perceptive Pooch were able to solve binomial equations, quadratics and, eventually, offer conclusive proof of Einstein's Special Theory.

Uncle Simon's dog act was different. His dog, Coco, used to produce turds shaped like letters of

My mother, Gladys. My parents put me onto the stage aged 4. By the age of 9 I had paid off their mortgage for them. They lost all interest in me after that

the alphabet. The audience would shout out their name and Coco would defecate their initials onto the stage, to a huge round of applause. On one memorable occasion – it was the night of the King's birthday in 1928 – Uncle Simon force-fed Coco with over thirty tins of dog-food an hour before the show. In return, Coco spelt out the entire National Anthem. There was an incredible round of applause, although the theatre emptied rapidly after that, due to the somewhat overpowering odour.

Father used to take me to the Variety Theatre in Blackgrind, where he went on Saturdays because a variety hall was the only place in the country you could see women's legs. (You wouldn't even see your own wife's in those days. We had proper morals then.) So, at a young age, I saw marvellous acts like the magician Grumpo the Amazing and the Highwire Brothers, who performed incredible acrobatics on a taut wire stretched ten feet above the stage (they lasted until 1936, when one of them fell and sliced himself in half). Then there was the comedian Melvyn Spickle – "A Song, A Smile and a Racist Remark" (these were the days before the Trendy Mafia moved in and told us what we were and weren't allowed to laugh at).

It was those wonderful occasions in the Variety Theatre at Blackgrind which made me resolve to go into show-business. My father did not take this particularly well – "'Appen tha's girl's blouse, at' ba' hermaphrodite," he said. However, when I had done a spot at Batskiggle Working Men's Club and earned five pounds for singing three Jack Buchanan songs, father began to support me, eventually becoming my unofficial manager and booking me seven shows a week, 52 weeks a year at only 85% commission. He and mother moved to a larger house and bought a motor car, but at that stage I was not bothered about money. I was too happy merely to be in show business.

At that time there were "youth revues" which toured the country. I auditioned for Jack Hylton's "Youth Takes a Bow", but failed to get in. However, I was accepted for Marius Dewby's "Cheap Child Labour", which toured the country to an audience of enthusiastic paedophiles. After that show I began working on my own in variety halls up and down the country. By 1939, at the age of nineteen, I was doing a solo comedy act, and was beginning to think myself quite a professional.

CHAPTER TWO:

Small Steps, Big Plans

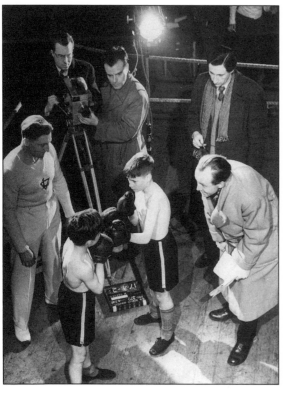

As a child actor, I took part in a number of British "B" features. This is a scene from "Young Boys in Shorts", which played a few select cinemas in Soho

I remember very well the day that war broke out. We all gathered around the radio in the lounge to hear Chamberlain's statement, and when he said, "I have to tell you that no such undertaking has been received, and that, conse-quently, this country is at war with Germany," my mother said, "Oh, dear – will we have time for lunch?"

Father rolled up his sleeves and went into the garden to begin construction of an air-raid shelter. He was at it all afternoon, with bricks, cement and corrugated iron. Eventually he came in and said to mother, "That'll stand anything but a direct hit." Then the cat jumped up on it to go to sleep and the whole thing collapsed. How we laughed!

I had a good war. For a start, two of my main rivals, Billy Custard and Tommy Grockley, both enlisted and got killed, so that was a major advance for my career. Tony Miggs, who was a gifted mimic and brilliant stand-up comedian, had his legs blown off in North Africa, which from my point of view was excellent. And when Cheeky Charlie Chippenham, my main rival for second-spot on the Hippodrome circuit, baled out over Belgium and found his parachute wasn't working, I was well on my way.

War wasn't all good times, though. I remember one time in 1942, I was due to close the first half at the prestigious Alhambra Theatre in Sparnley when there was an air-raid and the theatre suffered a direct hit. Fourteen people were killed, including five stagehands and my own dresser, and it was a very sad occasion from my point of view: first-half closing spots were not easy to come by, and now it looked as though it would be a long wait for another one. As I lay in my lodgings that night, listening to the groans of the people next door whose house had collapsed around their heads, I reflected that the Luftwaffe were probably planning their whole campaign around preventing me from finding success.

But a true show-biz trouper never gives up, and the next day I was offered a new chance. My call-up papers arrived at my parents', and keen though I was to fight for King and Country, I also felt that it would not be fair to deprive future generations of my immense talent merely to provide one more expendable soldier for Jerry to have a pop at. Naturally I fully supported our Forces in their gallant efforts to repel the fearsome tide of oppression and Nazi dictatorship that was threatening to engulf the whole of Europe, subjugating the free peoples of the world to a yoke of Fascist domination, but I felt that I would be better employed telling my jokes than actually fighting. Morale was, after all, vital to the troops, and nothing on earth would persuade me to die before I'd made it to the top in show business. (Although I have "died" many times on stage! – "Dying" is show-business slang for "getting no laughs"! I have used that crack many times at the show-business parties I am always invited to because I am famous.)

I remember the day of my medical very well. I had returned to my parents' house and my mother said that she was very proud of me for going off to join the fighting. Father, too, expressed his delight and also said he was pleased that after all my "fairying about with theatrical woofters" I was at last feeling "bellicose and truculent". I went along to the Recruitment Centre at Brimsfield where I underwent an examination. Naturally, I was classified A1; I was very fit in those days and still am now. (People always think that show-business people are fat, lazy, overpaid and unhealthy, but many of them are not. They belong to very expensive health clubs and play tennis, drive powerboats and sail yachts. I don't make any bones about my money because I come from a poor background. I have earned every penny of my money – well, apart from the couple of million that Dodd, Gee and Feinberg made for me from my investments in the South Africa Police Pension Fund – and I enjoy spending it.)

Anyway, my Army medical was a bit of a hoot, because I had decided that, in order to get out of fighting, I would feign a major psychological neurosis. The Army Medical Officer was a bluff sort of fellow – "You're in the Army now, you big namby-pamby theatrical whoopsie," he kept saying – and he quickly gave me all my tests. I had toyed with the idea of giving myself an asthma attack by rubbing myself with a cat just before going in, but in the end I decided that it would be better to pretend to be a severe schizophrenic depressive with agoraphobia. (I got the idea from a music-hall turn called Lottie McDottie, who used to do several "characters" during her act, including "Maysie the char-lady", "Davinia the tipsy Duchess", and "Prudence the schizophrenic depressive with agoraphobia".)

The Army chappie fell for my act. "Agoraphobic, eh?" he said. "Fat lot of use you'll be to the infantry." I agreed with this, thinking how clever I was. Two days later a letter arrived telling me I had been drafted for service on board a submarine, HMS *Rusty,* in the North Atlantic. This was bad news, for, while not at all agoraphobic, I am genuinely claustrophobic. (Years later, when I was flying on Concorde, which I do a lot because I am rich and successful, I felt very claustrophobic, but my wife snapped me out of it by saying, "For four grand a ticket you'd better bloody enjoy yourself." I had not realised the tickets had cost £4000 each, and fainted. I am not a mean man – I enjoy spending my money. But only on myself. That's my upbringing coming out. I remember my mother used to say "A penny spent is penny a'bart nowt t'spend more t'en bothik'." That's an old Northern dialect expression; it means, roughly, "I am a stingy bastard".)

Naturally, then, the prospect of serving on board a submarine did not appeal to me. In fact, to quote another favourite expression of my mother's, I shat a brick. I am not a cowardly man – my war-service record is as exemplary as you can get without actually fighting – but to be honest I'd rather open first house at the Glasgow Empire than serve on a submarine under the North Atlantic. So, using my tremendous talent for invention, or as my mother would put it, "lying", I wrote a letter saying that my agoraphobia had been miraculously cured, but I now had such severe claustrophobia that confinement within a submarine would result in psychotic violence. It worked! I was assigned to the Army, the 3rd Royal Bombardiers, and went off for Basic Training.

Basic Training took place at a camp in Hampshire. Our NCO was Sergeant "Mad Dog" Barker, and he was a bit of a Tartar! I quickly made friends with a chap called Harry Purkiss, because he was witty, quick and clever. I thought we'd make a pair of good chums, and, more to the point, I thought I might be able to steal some of his jokes and use them in my stage act. Purkiss had no thought whatsoever of going into show business – in fact, he worked in a bank in Bristol – and I thought I might try to persuade him to give it a whirl. He was naturally very funny, and did hilarious take-offs of the camp's officers, and he could also sing. At the last minute I realised he was considerably more talented than me, and kept my mouth shut. After the war, he went back to Bristol, to rot in obscurity. I used several of his jokes and voices in my act for many years, so he at least has some vague connection with fame and success which perhaps will comfort him in his dotage.

There was another chap there at the same time as me called Pinkerton, who was from the West Country, and had a very strong accent. He was very slow and rather dim and used to say, "I'd sooner be farmin'" whenever we were on exercises. He was hilarious, and I wanted to use him as a character for a radio show. But, of course, I would have had to get his permission and pay him royalties. However, one day, he mistook a live land-mine for a dummy one, so that problem was solved. I played him in the BBC's *Calling*

All Tommies in 1944, and, with his "I'd sooner be farmin'" catchphrase, I became so popular that I was able to do a variety tour based on him. On that tour I was earning nearly eight hundred pounds a week. Very soon I was so rich, I almost sent a tenner to his widow. Fortunately, I went to visit my parents just in time and my mother stopped me. "Don't be a daft booger," she said. "Tha's in't clover, and hang seng mo't' rest."

It was around this time that I began to hear of a young chap doing the rounds of the Forces entertainment circuit called Peter Sellers. He came from North London and did an act consisting of voices and impressions which, to be honest, were really not that good. I remember years later, when Sellers was known as the "Man of a Thousand Voices" and became a huge star in *The Goon Show,* that I turned to my wife and said "He's not really very good, actually, you know."

In 1965, when Sellers was a huge international star in the wake of films like *Dr Strangelove* and *What's New Pussycat?,* I met him outside the Hilton in Park Lane. We chatted in star-to-star camaraderie about the old days. "You've done alright for yourself then, Peter, mate," I said. He made a jocular comment about

On the set of ny first starring film, "Watch Those Clippers!" I played Ivor Brush, a funny barber. The film is still frequently shown on cable TV, usually around 5am

not having the faintest idea who I was, and said he was meeting Britt Ekland in five minutes. I was myself en route to the studio, to film a very prestigious commercial for Can-o-Krunch dog biscuits, so we parted as friends who had both ascended the show-business ladder to the same lofty heights.

When Peter died, in 1980, I remembered my first glimpse of him in 1944. Immediately, I phoned up the producers of all the TV news programmes. You get at least eighty quid an interview if you know someone who's just snuffed it.

After my immense success in *Calling All Tommies,* I was invited to take part in a new radio show called *Bang Goes the Meringue.* At the time the great favourite was Tommy Handley's *ITMA,* which I secretly thought was rubbish, principally because I wasn't in it. *ITMA* went from strength to strength, with its huge listenership and immense popularity, while *Bang Goes the Meringue* was cancelled after one programme. This was no doubt due to some conspiracy by rival comics, jealous of my talent, who wished to prevent me from rising up the show-business ladder. But you can't keep a good dog down, and soon I was offered a part in another radio show – *Ted On Arrival,* starring Ted Winsome, the "Housewives' Choice". Ted was hugely popular, handsome and sang songs as well as doing comedy. I saw, at once, that he was fundamentally untalented and had only got where he was by fluke.

My part on the show was as Tea-Pot Charlie – a character who came in every week to give Ted his cup of tea. It was only half-way through the first recording that I became aware that Tea-Pot Charlie *had no lines.* Given that this was radio, this was something of a drawback. I was there solely to get laughs from the studio audience; in other words, to prop up the useless star of the show until such time as he could get back to the pub, where he liked to drink himself insensible and then go home and beat up his wife. If she was his wife. I wouldn't have put anything past Ted Winsome. It seemed terribly unjust to me that an immoral, bad-tempered and thoroughly nasty chap like him could have a show of his own on the radio, while I was reduced to playing his stooge. I strongly suspected that his father was probably on the BBC Board of Governors.

After a few weeks, I worked out a way of increasing my part in the show. My idea was simple but, typical of me, it was utterly brilliant. I decided that I would make Tea-Pot Charlie an asthmatic. In the next week's show, when I came to the microphone with Ted's cup of tea, I wheezed very loudly on my way over, and then on my way back again. The audience were in stitches – this was the 1940s, after all, when jokes about disabling illnesses were not forbidden by the Trendy Gestapo – and after the show, Ted reacted predictably. "That was great!" he said. "You got a great laugh. Why don't you keep it in next week?" This was precisely the sort of generous, paternal response which left me secure in the knowledge that over the next few months I could upstage Ted completely and get him sacked.

This I set out to do. I worked out a way to wheeze popular tunes, so that every week Tea-Pot Charlie would give an asthmatic version of a popular hit as he delivered the tea. Then I decided to develop the character still further, and Tea-Pot Charlie became the world's first asthmatic impressionist. I still had no lines, but I had a repertoire of impressions of what different famous people would have sounded like if they had had a severe bronchial condition. The big favourite, of course, was Churchill. I wheezed the whole of "We will fight them on the beaches" one week, and got a huge round of applause. Afterwards, Ted generously told me it was one of the funniest things he had ever heard. I thanked him, and resolved that he would be on the dole within three months.

Finally, bowing to the inevitable, Ted Winsome was moved to a different programme – *Dead With Ted,* which was broadcast evenings on the Home Service, and in which Ted would read out requests from recently bereaved people. This was, effectively, the end of his career: three years later he would be reading the weather on the Third Programme, and a year after that he was to die of liver cirrhosis. I read one of the lessons at his funeral, and like to think that he counted me amongst his very best friends.

By 1950, I was a star. It had been a long, hard slog up the greasy pole of show business, but I had finally made it. The show-business mountain is steep, and there's not much room at the summit, so if you can get there without being swept away by the avalanche of fashion or carried off by the Yeti of criticism, then enjoy the view while you can. I wasn't to know it then, but you may not be there for very long.

For fame is a fickle mistress. When you are on top of the tree, there are many lesser people gathered around below, trying to shake you off. I remember my friend Tony Hancock once saying to me, "We nearly cast you as an extra in the library in *The Missing Page,* but we didn't." Tony was a dear, dear friend, and I remember seeing him, a struggling bottom-of-the-bill comic in 1948, and thinking how one of his routines might be worth nicking. Many years later, when he had found massive fame and was the best-known and richest comedian in Britain, I remember thinking "damn". In 1968, when a mixture of vodka and barbiturates ended his life in an Australian bedroom, I shed a brief tear, and then got on the phone to all the chat-show producers.

CHAPTER THREE:

Big Success, Bigger Head

1951 saw the first broadcast of my own series on the Home Service, *Who's Dropped One?* The show rapidly became incredibly popular, although, for various reasons, mostly to do with envy and jealousy, it doesn't tend to get talked about much today. It was recorded at the Palace Theatre in Camden, London, and was ground-breaking in many ways. We had a resident band, the Tony Bovis Quartet, and a resident announcer, Graham Triffid, whose droll introductions to the show each week became such a firm favourite with the audience that, eventually, I bowed to the inevitable and had him sacked.

I did all my favourite characters, including the rustic idiot who said "I'd rather be farmin'" whenever there wasn't a joke in the script; the brilliant Brigadier Gruffley-Plinge, with his "at ease there!" catchphrase (a character subsequently stolen by many other comedians who have never acknowledged their theft) and, of course, the Reverend Wiffle-Waffle, whose catchphrase, "Get out your hassocks, missus," was a national institution. (That character was blatantly stolen by Alan Bennett and his smart University friends for their intellectual-political revue *Beyond the Fringe,* which in my opinion marked the death of working-class, grass-roots, salt-of-the-earth comedy in Britain. Naturally, all the university-educated Mafia who run the media would disagree with this. But I can think of no other reason why a genius like myself should not have been employed by any television station for twenty years, apart from my appearance on the *News at Ten* when I was bankrupted. Oh, and a segment on *Without Walls* called "Sad As You Like: The Forgotten Men of Yesteryear." I didn't see it, but friends told me I came out of it very well.)

Anyway, back in the early Fifties, I was on top of the world. I moved from my flat in Notting Hill to a big house in Kent. The house was called Recherche du Temps Perdu, which Jemima and I universally decided wasn't really to our taste. We re-named it Squirrel's Holt and moved in. Naturally all the middle-class types that lived nearby were very envious that a working-class Northern boy should have been able to afford such a house. Evidently they felt that show-business types were not welcome in their stuffy world and I found I couldn't join the golf club or the tennis club on the grounds that I was "too common". That was Britain in the Fifties — still class-ridden and hidebound with prejudice and snobbery. This is the Britain which has so sadly disappeared nowadays. At least you knew where you were with it.

I have never made any secret of the way I vote. My father and his father before him were solid Labour supporters all their lives, but that was because they were just miners, with no God-given talent to get them out of the pit and into the luxurious high-life that is the privilege of those whom God has blessed with the gift of entertaining. I always supported Margaret Thatcher and thought she was a marvellous woman. Once, at a BBC Christmas party, I had an argument with Tom Benson, the foul-mouthed yobbish "alternative comedian" who, together with all his other university-educated chums, has driven real entertainers from the screen. Benson told me that, "he would not personally ever have performed at the Conservative Party Conference", and I told him to mind his own business. He then said, "but it's a free country and everyone has a right to their own opinion", and I told him to piss off and talk to his Stalinist friends.

The foul tongues and intolerant opinions of these young people make me weep for the England we've lost. Whatever happened to gentleness, decency, kindness, red telephone boxes, cricket on the village green, the tanned labourer munching his rosy apple as he rests after harvesting the golden wheat in the mellow glow of an English sunset? Whatever happened to the British bobby, Muffin the Mule, the Home Service, community spirit, the coal-man? What, in short, happened to the England that I once knew? Is this just hopeless nostalgia for a "golden age" that never was? No, I think it is more to do with the fact that I am not famous any more. I look at the yobbish, slobbish youths that I see slouching through the ugly "shopping precincts" that blight every town in this country, and I think to myself — could these drug-addled, lazy, ignorant teenage dropouts have gone up in a Lancaster and flown the Channel in pitch-darkness, with enemy flak flying and Messerschmidts on their tails, to save their country from oppression and tyranny? I do not think so. I think they would have announced that they "couldn't be bothered", and gone back to playing their video games and listening to the mindless thudding they call "music". Sometimes I seriously think about emigrating, perhaps to Australia.

It is true that I did once do cabaret at the Conservative Party Conference. In fact, it was the only paid gig I was offered in the 1980s. I was privately told that neither the BBC nor ITV would offer me a series because I was actually too funny, and would show up all the rest of their mediocre "stars" for the talentless rabble that they were. In any case, I should not have taken up their offer, even if they had made me one, for I was far too busy on other projects. I had already written one novel, *Greasepaint and Tears,* which was very nearly published. The publisher told me it was "barely disguised autobiography seething with bitterness and pathetic grudges", which was a remarkably perceptive assessment and which I took as a major compliment.

I have devoted a good deal of my time to my second novel, *The Forgotten Genius,* which I am still writing. My friends tell me – and I say this in all modesty – that it is "very long indeed".

But to return to the 1950s, the world was my oyster. *Who's Dropped One?* went from strength to strength, until in 1954 I was told that every Thursday night landlords were complaining that their pubs were emptying early so people could hear the show! At 9pm, every Thursday night, the streets would fall silent, buses would stop, factory shifts clock off, surgeons would leave patients in mid-operation to bleed to death while *Who's Dropped One?* was on the radio in the staff rest-room. The peak came on December 23rd, when the audience figure was reported as 55 million – the entire population of Great Britain!

But, at this peak of artistic and popular success, something was worrying me, nagging insistently at my brain. It was not enough, this fame and success and wealth. It was not enough, for the simple reason that Britain is, when you come down to it, a very small country. When I was a lad, sitting in the 3d. seats at the Cleckiemorple Hippodrome, the glamour of the silver screen was the glamour of Hollywood. In my mid-teens I saw Robert Donat in *The Thirty-Nine Steps,* and in my dreams I too was chained to Madeleine Carroll. Or rather, I was chained, and Madeleine Carroll was standing over me, dressed in full Nazi uniform. But we won't go into that here. I don't approve of these nasty biographies that are full of salacious dirt. I feel that, for a wholesome show-business personality like myself, the public want to know about my successes, my ups and downs, and my happy family life, and not about my alcoholism, my secret visits to Soho massage parlours and my childhood molestation by my Uncle Arthur. Those sorts of things didn't happen in those days. Well, they did, but not to me. And even if they had, I wouldn't write about them.

I phoned up my agent, Hugh Jaffee, and told him I wanted to go into movies. He told me I was daft, that I had a good career here and should stick with it. His exact words were, "You're off your bleeding trolley, you go away for six months and the bastards'll forget all about you, plus you're far too ugly." But I was not to be dissuaded so easily. Looking back on it, I can see my decision was a mistake. A tragic, crazy, stupid, mad mistake that plunged me into decades of misery, despair, alcoholism and failure, taking me to Stygian depths of suicidal, nihilistic depression.

But it seemed a good idea at the time, plus I have an ego the size of Andrew Lloyd-Webber's deposit account. So to Hollywood I went.

CHAPTER FOUR:

Big Mistake, Huge Cock-Up

Punto & Dennisovitch; last of the variety-hall pyscho-jugglers

Hollywood in the 1950s was an extraordinary place. The "golden era" was, perhaps, already over, and television was making great inroads into the movie audience, so that the craze was for big, wide-screen spectaculars that would pull people back into the movie houses.

One such spectacular was in production at the Mayberg-Thalwyn Studio – *Caesar and Boadicea*, a historical epic set in Britain, about a romance between the warlike Queen of the Britons and the Roman general. Arriving on location, I was surprised to see Roman East Anglia dotted with palm trees. I was also surprised to see that Boadicea intended going into battle against the full might of the Roman army in a low-cut dress and with her hair loose.

My part was to be Dronkio, a comic slave who, in the script, had 38 lines. On my arrival I found that these had been cut down to one – "I am slain." Naturally, I was a trifle annoyed by this, but I discovered that the film's star, James Korneye, had demanded my part be cut because I was too funny and he was afraid that I would steal the picture. I chatted to the actress playing Boadicea, Jane Trowell, a gorgeous American girl who was being groomed for stardom and had already been given major roles by several senior executives, although this was her first actual acting job. She found me irresistible, with my English charm and my accent. Jane and I made passionate love in her trailer every lunchtime. She was an incredible lover, but then so am I. When the director found out about our steamy affair I was fired from the picture. I was annoyed by this, as I had made it all up.

176

I met James Stewart one night in the Polo Lounge. He was a favourite of mine, and we had a few drinks and I complimented him on his marvellous performance in *Rear Window.* Then we had a few more drinks, and I asked him about Hitchcock and the shooting of *Rear Window.* Then we had a few more drinks, and I asked him whether Grace Kelly's tits were as amazing as they looked. He rose and left, and I never saw him again.

On another, memorable occasion, I chanced to meet Orson Welles in the Brown Hat one night. He was in town trying to raise money for a new picture. We had a few drinks, and I complimented him on his marvellous performance in *The Third Man.* We had a few more drinks, and I asked him about the studio re-editing of *The Magnificent Ambersons.* Then we had a few more drinks, and I asked him whether Rita Hayworth's tits were as fabulous as they looked. He walked out, and I never saw him again.

I found Hollywood people cold, and rude. For a down-to-earth man like myself, I find that sort of behaviour very hard to take. I began to become homesick for Ty-Phoo tea, warm beer, and most of all, fame and success.

In the mid-Fifties, in the wake of the McCarthy trials, a host of "invasion" movies were made, playing on America's pet phobia, the spectre of Communism. The most famous of these, *Invasion of the Bodysnatchers,* inspired a host of imitations. I was offered a part in one of these, a film called *It Came from Uranus.* It was an unfortunate title (although I thought it was extremely funny!), but the producers said that every other planet had now been used, and Uranus was the only one left. There had been *The Invaders From Mercury, Venus Invades Earth, Invaders from Mars, They Came From Saturn, Invasion From Planet Jupiter, Neptune Invaders,* and *Earth Invades Earth by Mistake.* That only left Uranus; another studio had conducted market research to find out why *The Terror from Pluto* had flopped dismally at the box-office, and found that the public's knowledge of astronomy was not extensive, and that they had thought it was a horror-film about a cartoon dog. So *It Came from Uranus* it was. I was offered the part of Third Scientist, and had one line – "I am slain."

The film received derisory reviews. "The puerile title says it all," said one. "An appalling, schoolboy double-entendre on a lavatorial level. I predict a smash-hit in Britain."

I took this as a great compliment.

I was next offered the part of Charred Corpse in *Mutants Must Die,* and decided that it was obviously time to go home.

CLASSIC FICTION

A Sherlock Holmes Mystery

The Adventure of 221c

SIR ARTHUR CONAN DOILY

Chapter One

It was, as I recall, in the winter of 1893 that my friend Sherlock Holmes and I became embroiled in one of the most singular cases we were ever called upon to deal with. Holmes had been idle ever since his success in unravelling the conundrum of the Unshaven Chemist, and, apart from assisting in the recovery of the Figgis-Snetterton Plans (thus saving for Britain the patent on the most advanced kitchen-ventilation equipment then available) and solving the labyrinthine complexities surrounding the murder of Sir Roger Parkes (the naval attaché found with his navel attached to a ship's propeller off Finisterre), he had been in a state of indolent melancholy all autumn. 221b Baker Street was a sorry apartment indeed, as the strains of Holmes' violin filled the air – slow, lugubrious Bach when my friend was thinking, until a frenetic burst of Rimski-Korsakov would announce that he had once again been at his cocaine.

One evening, I arrived back at 221b to find our landlady showing a woman around the hall. The woman was unknown to me, but her countenance was pleasing, not to say handsome.

"Ah, Dr Watson," began the landlady, with whom I had not spoken recently, following a slight altercation over Holmes' use of various fixtures and fittings as weapons in subduing Josiah Madd at the conclusion of the Adventure of the Psychopathic Newsagent. "Pray, let me introduce Miss Marilyn Worstenholme. She and a companion will henceforth be renting 221c Baker Street. I hope and trust that yourself and Mr Holmes will prove yourselves good neighbours."

Holmes was pacing the study when I arrived, clutching his violin in an agitated state.

"It is a source of great disappointment to me, Watson," he cried, "that the violin is perceived by the public as such a high-falutin' instrument, beloved only of the highly cultured, and sneered at by the masses. Surely it would be possible to popularise it? Surely someone could be found – someone who, if necessary, could feign a Cockney accent, spike their hair and talk with a lisp?" His eyes sparkled, but dimmed again. "No – it is an absurd notion, Watson. Now – have you managed to get me any decent shit?"

"I have not," I replied with dignity. "Your dependence on artificial stimulants is something which I, as a doctor..."

"Oh, fiddlesticks, Watson!" came the reply. "Pray, do not lecture me. Like poets and writers, I live by my observation and my brain. Do people refuse to read Coleridge, or de Quincey, for their use of opium? Then why should a detective not feed his mind in the same way?"

"Because in your last investigation you arrested a chest-of-drawers. If the Lord had intended us to use drugs..."

"If the Lord had *not* intended us to use drugs, my dear Watson, he would have made a world that was bearable without them. But let us desist from such wrangling. How goes the metropolis? What nefarious capers require my talents? Which sordid manifestations of human wickedness need my utmost attention?"

"You mean, has anyone been bumped off today?"

"Indeed, Watson, you have hit the nail so squarely on the head as to drive it clean through the wood and out the other side. Has anyone been bumped off today? Is the capital littered with corpses? Are its streets and thoroughfares blocked with stiffs, its left-luggage offices stacked with suspiciously malodorous trunks? For nothing could make me happier."

"Afraid not," I said. "No murders today."

"Ah," sighed Holmes, laying down his Stradivarius. "It is an evil sign of the times, Watson, a symptom of an enfeebled and decadent *zeitgeist*, when the homicides cease. All great, powerful, healthy societies are full of murder. Think through history, Watson. The Roman Empire – murders galore, even Emperors. Renaissance Italy – deaths a-plenty. Elizabethan England – safe? Tell that to Christopher Marlowe. Revolutionary France? They were dropping *comme les mouches*. Even our own age, the age of Victoria, the zenith of Empire, has been accompanied by the numerous slayings which attest to the spirit, cunning and drive of a great people. Think, Watson, think! – of the mental agility required by a great poisoner; the guts and strength needed to accomplish a stabbing; the intimate study of anatomy, mass-to-weight ratios and structural stress prerequisite upon a successful hanging. These are the same qualities that made us great, Watson. I fear for England when its citizens no longer seethe with the desire to slip strychnine into each other's cocoa."

"I believe you need a rest, Holmes," I said. "You are talking almost treasonably. All murderers are fiends, fit only for the gallows."

"It is for your liberal opinions that I value you so highly, Watson," replied Holmes. "For you must understand that murder is my livelihood. I depend on it, as a publican depends on beer."

"Well, I am afraid that there have been no murders of late, and I, for one, rejoice in it."

"Then my mind remains idle, Watson, and shall do until someone is found spattered all over the London to Brighton line, or dangling from Admiralty Arch with a carrot up each nostril." (Holmes' astonishing

Holmes enjoyed playing psychopaths at chess

premonitory powers were to be proved the following year, when we found ourselves drawn into the Adventure of the Man Found Dangling from Admiralty Arch with a Carrot up each Nostril.)

My friend stalked the room for a while, clearly upset that none of London's citizens had met a grisly end, thus providing him with something to do. Neither of us realised, however, that events were about to begin which would provide a far more singular investigation than any murder we had ever encountered.

It began later that same night. It was getting fairly late, and I was preparing to retire to bed, although Holmes was busy setting up some test-tubes and retorts for a chemical experiment he wished to conduct. Suddenly, both of us became aware of a low, moaning noise, slightly indistinct. It sounded like an animal at first, but, as we attuned our ears, the noise became recognisably human.

"What on earth is that, Holmes?"

"Very singular, Watson," replied my friend. "It sounds indubitably like a man in some pain, and it appears to be emanating from upstairs."

"But there are only two ladies upstairs," I replied. "Miss Worstenholme and her companion."

"Most odd," replied Holmes. "Anyway, Watson, I must continue with this experiment." So saying, he took a large pair of scissors and cut one of his shirts clean in two.

"Whatever are you doing, Holmes?"

"Ah, you may well enquire, Watson. You see, ordinary powders leave behind the really stubborn stains at forty degrees, so I intend washing one half of the shirt in our normal powder, but the other half in concentrated nitric acid."

I did not follow this at all, so I said goodnight and went to bed. Before I went to sleep I thought I could hear more groans from upstairs, but I was so tired that I was asleep before I could be sure.

Chapter Two

"I told you a visit to Texas Homecare would be worthwhile, Watson"

It was a couple of days later that the dung really hit the fan, as we used to say in the Army. Holmes and I were consuming an excellent breakfast when Holmes looked up from the morning paper with a grave look in his eye.

"The foul breath of scandal looks set to afflict the national nose," he said. "Look at this, on the front page of the *Daily Bulletin*."

He handed me the journal, and I perused the story which Holmes had indicated. It ran thus:

"TITTLE-TATTLE OF MINISTER'S MISDOINGS – All Westminster is currently Agog with Rumour concerning a Minister of the Crown, whose Identity is currently a closely contrived Secret, and shall remain so on Our Part, though other, more scurrilous Publications shall doubtless venture the Name, baseless though the Allegations against him are said to Be. The Allegations in Question, Baseless though they are, do not need to be enumerated here for mere Public Titillation, but as a matter of Record it is our Duty to set them down. It appears that the Minister in question has, on sundry and diverse occasions of late been in the company of Ladies of questionable Virtue from whom he has been in receipt of certain Services, which it is not in the nature of this Newspaper to divulge. The Minister in question has Denied all the Allegations, which are in any case Baseless."

"Good heavens, Holmes," I expostulated. "Who would have thought it?"

"I suspect the work of agitators," muttered Holmes. "Agents of the Kaiser, or some Balkan power intent on making mischief. I do believe,

Watson, that here may be a case, at last, which will exercise my mental muscle to its fullest capacity."

This thought excited Holmes so much that he abandoned his eggs and gammon and returned to his chemical bench, there to examine the results of his recent experiment.

"It is as I suspected, Watson," he cried after examining the two halves of the shirt. "You see? With the normal powder those really stubborn stains remain – you see there, some blood, a relic of the Adventure of the Haemophiliac Knife-Grinder, and down there, some spatters of distinctive South Devonshire mud remaining from our little tussle at the end of the Adventure of the Irritating Rambler. But see here! With concentrated nitric acid, the stains have vanished."

"True, Holmes," I said. "But so has the shirt."

"Precisely, Watson. From this we can learn something of acid-bath murderers, but quite what we can learn, I do not know. Now – to business."

For the rest of the day Holmes sat in his favourite armchair, slumped in thought. Indeed, I had not seen him so engrossed since the Adventure of the Dismembering Plumber, where he had puzzled out how the murderer, who had removed the limbs of his victim and smuggled them out of his house in lengths of pipe, had only ever been seen doing so three times and not the four times one would expect. Holmes deduced that the victim had been either one-legged or one-armed, and proved absolutely correct. I may some day write up the Adventure of the Three-Pipe Problem.

It was another of Holmes' brilliant disguises

Around mid-afternoon, a knock came at the door.

"Aha!" cried Holmes. "A client! Someone with an appalling problem for me to solve!"

I rushed to the door, and there stood a small, middle-aged man who wore spectacles and slightly shabby clothing.

"Come in, dear Sir!" cried Holmes. "Don't tell me – wife disappeared? Wife murdered? Brother murdered? Death threats? Mysterious satsuma pips in the post? Whatever it is, come in and tell me about it."

The gentleman seemed unwilling to step inside, and stared about him somewhat sheepishly.

"Er – are you Babette?" he asked, finally.

"Quite wrong," cried Holmes.

"Is this the right address for… services?"

"Indeed!" I beamed. "Mr Holmes here is too modest to admit it, but his services have been enjoyed by some of the crowned heads of Europe."

This seemed to shock the man, and his jaw fairly dropped.

"Really?" he croaked.

"Oh, yes," I continued. "Many a great personage has made their way to Baker Street, and left fully satisfied."

"Really, Watson, you flatter me too much," said Holmes. "Invite the gentleman in, for in truth, Sir, it is some time since we have had a client."

183

The chap now seemed extremely flustered. "This is 221c Baker Street?" he asked.

"No, no," I replied, a trifle annoyed. This is 221b. Flat C is upstairs."

"Thank Christ for that," said the man. I was shocked by his profanity. He blushed a deep red, and then scampered upstairs.

"This is all distinctly odd, Watson," said Holmes, obviously disappointed at having been let down. "For did you not tell me that the occupant upstairs is called Marilyn Worstenholme? Then who is this 'Babette?'"

"Evidently, that must be her companion," I replied.

"Again, distinctly strange, Watson. The name would suggest a French lady, and I would venture to suggest that our good landlady would be most unlikely to let one of her rooms to a foreigner. Indeed, I seem to recall she would not let it to anyone Welsh, let alone French."

Our discussion was interrupted at this point by the arrival of the first edition of the evening paper. The front page was full of further news of the scandal.

"I have been distracted from this by our strange visitor, Watson. I must direct my thoughts back to this poor Minister, whose career, it seems, is so endangered by sinister middle-European forces."

As Holmes pondered the problem I happened to glance through the window and noticed a Hansom cab pulling up in the street outside.

"Great heavens, Holmes!" I cried, as I espied the personage disembarking therefrom. "You were correct!"

Holmes rushed to the window, and we watched as a certain Minister of the Crown in Her Majesty's Government paid off the driver of the Hansom and, with an anxious glance around him, headed towards our front door.

"It is as I thought," said Holmes. "The poor man, at the end of his tether, is coming here to consult with me. Make ready, Watson – I daresay he will be in quite a state."

I plumped a few cushions and checked all the decanters, and the two of us listened as the tread upon the stair grew louder. It then grew softer again.

"That is very strange," I commented. "He appears to have gone upstairs."

"Most singular," replied Holmes. "Perhaps he has mistaken our address."

But apparently no mistake had been made, for the Minister did not return to our floor. We heard the door upstairs open; and then all was silence.

"All rather curious, Watson," said Holmes, once again disappointed in his hope that his keen brain might be required.

It was a few minutes later that the strange groaning began once again.

Motor-racing was only Nigel Mansell's second choice of career

"Listen!" cried Holmes.

I listened, and my blood ran cold. For from upstairs were emanating the unmistakable sounds of a fearsome beating. The moans were louder than ever.

"I was right, Watson!" whispered Holmes. "This Miss Worstenholme is nothing more than a front for sinister Eastern European subversives. Even now, one of our country's senior Ministers is being tortured! Who knows what State secrets he may divulge! Quick – we have no time to lose!"

With this, Holmes ran from the room. I took my trusty pistol from its case and followed him up the stairs. Holmes was already on the landing, crouched outside the door to 221c.

"Listen, Watson! The fiends! They have already wrung from him the name of the Head of Overseas Intelligence!"

Sure enough, from within could be heard cries of "Moore, Moore." Only three people in the whole country knew that Sir Nicholas Moore was the Head of Overseas Intelligence. Those three people were the Prime Minister, the Foreign Secretary, and Sherlock Holmes (the Queen had not been told, since the F.O. felt that having been married to a German made her a security risk).

"This is intolerable," muttered Holmes. "Stand back, Watson, and be ready with the pistol!"

With this, he laid his shoulder against the door and with a mighty shove we found ourselves inside the apartment. The sight which greeted our eyes will stay with me for ever. Miss Worstenholme and her companion were both standing, in bizarre apparel consisting largely of belts, and both were clutching horse-whips. The Minister, for his part, was lying on some strange contraption which seemed to be some sort of frame. His ankles and wrists had been shackled to the frame, and he was entirely unclothed apart from a school tie around his neck, and a small dunce's cap perched on his head.

"What is the meaning of this?" cried Holmes.

"What are you doing?" hissed Miss Worstenholme, turning to face us. She was sporting a pair of highly polished riding boots, and I noticed for the first time that, in her shock at the door being opened, a mortar-board had fallen from her head.

"What the devil are you playing at, you idiots? Shut the bloody door!" cried the Minister, his face beetroot-red.

"Do not panic, Sir," said Holmes, calmly. "My friend Dr Watson and I will have you free in no time, and these villains will be safely in the hands of Inspector Lestrade."

"Lestrade? Isn't he due at nine-thirty?" said Miss Worstenholme. Holmes and I exchanged puzzled glances.

"Do not worry," Holmes reassured the Minister. "We will have you free in no time at all."

"Piss off!" he responded, most ungraciously. "For heaven's sake. Ten guineas this cost me!"

"Which of you is Babette?" I asked.

"Babette?" said the Minister. "You told me your name was Nicole."

Miss Worstenholme walked across to a small table, her garments creaking noisily as she did so. On the table lay a small Kaiser's helmet, and a pile of cards, one of which she handed to me. I glanced at it. It read, "Naughty Boys Need Strict Mistress. West End. Telephone 23."

"You have a telephone?" I asked.

"Been a boon, love," replied Miss Worstenholme's companion.

"Do I understand," said Holmes slowly, "that gentlemen pay to be strapped to this contraption and struck with whips?"

"That's right."

"Very singular."

"I shall fetch the police at once, Holmes, " I said.

"What are you saying?" shouted the Minister, in panic.

"They're saying it's all over," said Worstenholme.

"It is now," groaned the Minister.

Chapter Three

Holmes was pacing the room with a puzzled expression. Eventually, he motioned me to follow him back downstairs. Once safely in our own room, Holmes lit a pipe. After a few minutes in which he puffed his way into a miasma of fumes, he spoke.

"Let us consider the facts, Watson. Firstly, there are reports of an incipient scandal at Westminster. Secondly, a Cabinet Minister appears at 221 Baker Street, apparently to consult me about this problem. Half an hour later he is discovered upstairs, shackled, obviously in some pain and yet most unwilling to be released from his predicament. What conclusions can we draw?"

I hesitated, but Holmes did not wait for my reply.

"Send a telegram to the Editor of the *Daily Flysheet*, Watson. Telegram to read: MP'S VICE-DEN SHOCKER STOP CALL GIRL TELLS ALL SHOCK HE TOLD ME NEVER TO STOP STOP." I looked at Holmes, but he just grinned.

"The thing us about us Victorians, Watson," he said, "is that we weren't as stupid as everyone thinks."